Copycat Recipes Making

American Cuisine 100+ Delicious Recipes The Complete Step-By-Step Guide for Making Your Favorite Restaurant Recipes at Home. From Appetizers to Desserts

Arsenio Islas

© Copyright 2020 by Arsenio Islas. All right reserved. The work contained herein has been produced with the intent to provide relevant knowledge and information on the topic on the topic described in the title for entertainment purposes only. While the author has gone to every extent to furnish up to date and true information, no claims can be made as to its accuracy or validity as the author has made no claims to be an expert on this topic. Notwithstanding, the reader is asked to do their own research and consult any subject matter experts they deem necessary to ensure the quality and accuracy of the material presented herein.

This statement is legally binding as deemed by the Committee of Publishers Association and the American Bar Association for the territory of the United States. Other jurisdictions may apply their own legal statutes. Any reproduction, transmission, or copying of this material contained in this work without the express written consent of the copyright holder shall be deemed as a copyright violation as per the current legislation in force on the date of publishing and subsequent time thereafter. All additional works derived from this material may be claimed by the holder of this copyright.

The data, depictions, events, descriptions, and all other information forthwith are considered to be true, fair, and accurate unless the work is expressly described as a work of fiction. Regardless of the nature of this work, the Publisher is exempt from any responsibility of actions taken by the reader in conjunction with this work. The Publisher acknowledges that the reader acts of their own accord and releases the author and Publisher of any responsibility for the observance of tips, advice, counsel, strategies, and techniques that may be offered in this volume.

Table of Contents

Introduction

Chapter 1: Breakfast Favorites

Apple Corn Muffins

Apple Pie Pull-Apart Bread With Vanilla Glaze

Banana Bread

Biscuits & Gravy

Cheddar Bay Biscuits

Eggs Benedict

Fried Apples

Lemon & Blueberry Ricotta Pancakes

Overnight Pumpkin Pie Oatmeal

Potato Waffles

Sausage Egg & Cheese Breakfast Sliders

Scrambled Eggs With Cream Cheese

Southern-Style Grits

Sweet Potato Muffins With Cinnamon Sugar Topping

Chapter 2: Poultry Favorites

Chicken & Dumplings

Crispy Oven-Fried Chicken

Crockpot Orange Chicken

Honey-Garlic Chicken

Mozzarella Stuffed Chicken Parm Quick & Easy Air Fryer Chicken Breast

Roasted Chicken With Pan Gravy

Chapter 3: Ground Beef Favorites

American Beef Goulash

Barbeque Burgers

Cheesy Fiesta Beef Casserole - Texas-Style

Chipotle Chili Sloppy Joes

Cincinnati Chili

Family Meatloaf

Glazed Bacon & Cheese Burgers

One-Skillet Shepherd's Beef Pie

Texas Beef Tacos

Worcestershire-Glazed Burgers

Chapter 4: Favorite Beef Cuts

Beef Stroganoff

Chicken-Fried Steak

Crockpot Pepper Steak

Philly Cheesesteak Sliders

Cheesesteak Quesadillas

Chapter 5: Seafood Favorites

Air Fryer Cod

Baked Catfish

Best Tuna Melt

Blackened Catfish Sandwich With Cabbage & Avocado

Connecticut-Style Lobster Roll

East Coast Shrimp & Lentil Bowls

Garlic Parmesan Flounder

Lemon Pan-Fried Trout

Maple Bacon Salmon

Old-Fashioned Salmon Patties

Oysters Rockefeller

Roasted Salmon

Rum-Glazed Shrimp

Chapter 6: Pork Favorites

Creamy Paprika Pork

Grilled Pork Chops With Smokin' Sauce

Mango-Glazed Ham On The Grill

No-Fuss Pork Chops

Peachy Pork Ribs

Pork Loin Steaks

Pork Medallions With Garlic-Strawberry Sauce

Southern-Style Pork Tenderloin Fajitas

Chapter 7: Pasta Favorites

Classic Baked Macaroni & Cheese

Elbow Macaroni & Vegetable Toss

Mason Jar Pasta Salad

New Orleans Sausage Shrimp Crawfish Pasta

Shrimp Monica - Original Crawfish & Noodles

Chapter 8: Salad Favorites

California Avocado Salad

California Quinoa Salad

Classic Chicken Salad

Classic Cobb Salad

Crab Louie Lettuce Wraps

Grilled Southwestern Pasta & Steak Salad

Southern Cornbread Salad

Southwestern Pork Salad

Waldorf Salad

Chapter 9: Soup Favorites

Best Ever Beef Stew - Slow-Cooked

Brunswick Stew

Cabbage Roll Soup

Cheeseburger Soup

Cheesy Ham Chowder

Creamy Chicken Noodle Soup - Slow-Cooked

Potato Beer Cheese Soup

Sausage & Chicken Gumbo - Slow-Cooked

Seafood Soup

Traditional New England Clam Chowder

Wild Rice Soup

Chapter 10: Bread & Side Dish Favorites

Easy Cornbread

Southern-Style Biscuits

Cauliflower Casserole

Curry With Cauliflower & Butternut Squash

Deviled Eggs

Grits n Greens

Marinated Tomatoes, Onions & Cucumbers

Northwoods Wild Rice Salad

Sausage & Mushroom Cornbread Dressing

Spicy Cajun Potato Salad

Turkey Pinto Bean Salad With Southern Molasses Dressing

Yukon Gold & Sweet Potato Gratin

Chapter 11: Veggie Favorites

Baked Sweet Onions

BBQ Beans

Creamed Corn - Crockpot
Garlic Mashed Potatoes
Green Beans With Garlic & Peppers
Grilled Mexican Corn
Honey Sage Carrots
Southern Fried Squash
Spicy Roasted Broccoli

Chapter 12: Pie Favorites
Pie Crust
Apple Pie
Big Boy Strawberry Pie
Blueberry-Custard Pie
Chess Pie
Coconut Cream Pie Bars
Creamy Hazelnut Pie
The Famous Woolworth Ice Box Cheesecake
Frozen Banana Split Pie
Frozen Peach Pie
Key Lime Pie
Strawberry Lemonade Freezer Pie
Sweet Potato Pie

Chapter 13: Cake Favorites
Blueberry Sour Cream Pound Cake

Carrot Cake Delight

Four Layer Pumpkin Cake With Frosting

Georgia Peach Pound Cake

Pineapple Pecan Cake With Frosting

Red Velvet Cake

Chapter 14: Other Sweet Goodies

American Patriotic Dessert Dish

Banana Pudding

Blackberry Cobbler

Blueberry-Peach Cobbler
Grandma's Divinity

Honey-Baked Apples

Pumpkin Butterscotch Pudding

Tennessee Peach Pudding

Conclusion

Get the audiobook version of this title for free with a 30-day Audible trial

Click here if you are from the US:
https://www.audible.com/pd/B08N5LXHPY/?source_code=AUDFPWS0223189MWT-BK-ACX0-221978&ref=acx_bty_BK_ACX0_221978_rh_us

Click here if you are from the UK:
https://www.audible.co.uk/pd/B08N5JH8KW/?source_code=AUKFrDlWS0223189OH6-BK-ACX0-221978&ref=acx_bty_BK_ACX0_221978_rh_uk

Click here if you are from the FR:
https://www.audible.fr/pd/B08N5KRKP4/?source_code=FRAORWS022318903B-BK-ACX0-221978&ref=acx_bty_BK_ACX0_221978_rh_fr

Click here if you are from the DE:
https://www.audible.de/pd/B08N5LJY8H/?source_code=EKAORWS0223189009-BK-ACX0-221978&ref=acx_bty_BK_ACX0_221978_rh_de

Introduction

Congratulations on purchasing the *American Cuisine,* and thank you for doing so. The following chapters will discuss a massive array of delicious recipes you can enjoy daily. If you are looking for delicious meals and desserts with easy to follow instructions; you have come to the right place. You will learn how to prepare dishes that your friends and family can enjoy anytime for many years to come!

You can choose from delicious breakfast dishes, beef, pork, seafood, pasta, and so much more. Enjoy healthy veggies and fruits by learning how to prepare a batch of unique desserts.

First, let's get the kitchen prepared with a few essential tools and other items. Check this out:

Instant-Read Digital Meat Thermometer: You can be sure your meats are thoroughly cooked according to your recipe if you have this handy gadget in your array of tools. For example, Walmart has one for around $10. If you are a beginner or just want to make sure your meats are safe to eat, the investment will pay for itself!

Accurate Measuring Tools: A measuring cup and spoon system that shows both the US and Metric standards of weight is essential, so there is no confusion during prep. If you are stocking your kitchen, it's also helpful to choose a clear container where you can easily view the contents of the recipe.

A Good Set of Scales: Portion control is essential for preparing your favorite meal or dessert. You want a scale that will accommodate your needs. Consider these options:

- *Seek a Conversion Button:* You need to know how to convert measurements into grams since not all recipes have them listed. The grams keep the system in complete harmony.

- *Removable Plate:* Keep the germs off of the scale by removing the plate to help eliminate a bacterial buildup.

- *The Tare Function:* When you set a bowl on the scale, the feature will allow you to reset the scale back to zero (0).

Sharp Knives: You will need a sharp knife for many of your meal options. You may want to invest in a sharpener at home. If your budget allows, purchase high-quality tools, and have them professionally sharpened annually.

Sifter: Purchase a good sifter for under $10, and you will be ensured a more accurate measurement for your cooking and baking needs. It will also save time when you are combining items, including flour, baking powder, sugar, etc.

Parchment paper will be used for a few of the recipes. The baking pans are lined with the paper so that the baked goods cannot stick. For most baking needs, you can omit the oils if you choose the paper. However, some recipes use paper and oils. It's another personal preference to save the mess and time!

These are just a few quick pointers so you can enjoy each of the delicious American Cuisine recipes to achieve the maximum result. You can add to your collection as time passes if you're a beginner. Consider what many of the pros suggest, purchase items that will maintain the test of time, but still consider your finances.

Thanks again for choosing this book, make sure to leave a short review if you enjoy it, I'd really love to hear your thoughts.

Chapter 1: Breakfast Favorites

Apple Corn Muffins

Servings Provided: 12
Time Required: 40 minutes

Ingredients Needed:

- Apple (1)
- All-purpose flour (2 cups)
- Packed brown sugar (.25 cup)
- Salt (.25 tsp.)
- Baking powder (1 tbsp.)
- Yellow cornmeal (.5 cup
- Egg whites (2)
- Fat-free milk (.75 cup)
- Corn kernels (.5 cup)
- Also Needed: 12-cup muffin pan

Preparation Technique:

1. Warm the oven to reach 425° Fahrenheit.
2. Peel and coarsely chop the apple.
3. Line the muffin cups and with foil or paper liners.
4. Mix the cornmeal, baking powder, flour, brown sugar, and salt in a mixing container.

5. Use a separate mixing bowl to whisk the egg whites, and add the milk. Blend in the apple bits and corn.
6. Whisk again and pour the batter into the flour mixture. Continue to stir the fixings until slightly moistened.
7. Dump the mixture into the cups (2/3 full). Set a timer to bake for about half an hour.
8. Test the muffins for doneness by gently pressing the center. They are done when they spring back.

Apple Pie Pull-Apart Bread With Vanilla Glaze

Servings Provided: 6-8
Time Required: 40 minutes

Ingredients Needed:

- Granulated sugar (.33 cup)
- Nutmeg (.25 tsp.)
- Cinnamon (1 tsp.)
- Pillsbury Grands Flaky Layers Biscuits (16 oz.)
- Thinly sliced medium apple (1)
- Cooking oil spray (as needed)

  Ingredients - The Glaze:

- Vanilla extract (.25 tsp.)
- Milk (1.5 tbsp.)

Preparation Technique:

1. Set the oven temperature at 350° Fahrenheit.
2. Prepare a loaf pan with a layer of parchment baking paper. Spray lightly with the cooking oil spray.
3. Whisk the cinnamon, sugar, and nutmeg in a shallow dish and set aside for now.
4. Take the biscuits out of the container and slice into halves. Break the dough into 16 rounds.
5. Coat each of the apple slices and round of biscuit dough with the cinnamon and sugar mixture. Layer into the pan, alternating the

rounds, beginning with the biscuit on the bottom, and end on the top.
6. Bake until the bread is done throughout or approximately 35-45 minutes.
7. Prepare the vanilla glaze. Combine all the ingredients in a medium mixing container and drizzle over the warm baked bread.

Banana Bread

Servings Provided: 16
Time Required: 15 minutes

Ingredients Needed:

- Baking powder (1 tsp.)
- Stevia (.25 tsp.)
- Xanthan gum (.5 tsp.)
- Salt (.5 tsp.)
- Almond flour (.75 cup)
- Coconut flour (.33 cup)
- Vanilla extract (1 tsp.)
- Medium eggs (6)
- Erythritol (.5 cup)
- Coconut oil (3 tbsp.)
- Medium banana (1)
- Melted butter (.5 cup)

Preparation Technique:

1. Set the oven temperature setting at 325° Fahrenheit. Grease a loaf pan.
2. Combine the almond and coconut flour with the xanthan gum, stevia, salt, erythritol, and baking powder.
3. Slice the banana and add to a food processor with the butter, oil, eggs, and vanilla extract. Pulse it for one minute and combine it with the remainder of the fixings.
4. Pulse one more minute until well blended. Dump the batter into the loaf pan and bake for

1 ¼ hours. Enjoy for breakfast or a snack anytime!

Biscuits & Gravy

Servings Provided: 8
Time Required: 15 minutes

Ingredients Needed:

The Biscuits:
- Baking powder (1 tsp.)
- Almond flour (1 cup)
- Celtic sea salt (.25 tsp.)
- Egg whites (4)
- Organic butter or cold coconut oil (2 tbsp.)
- Optional: Garlic or another preferred spice (1 tsp.)

The Gravy:
- Chicken or beef broth (1 cup)
- Cream cheese (1 cup)
- Ground black pepper (1 pinch)
- Celtic sea salt (as desired)
- Organic crumbled pork sausage (10 oz. pkg.)

Preparation Technique:

1. Set the oven temperature at 400º Fahrenheit. Prepare a muffin pan or cookie tray using an oil baking spray.
2. Chop the butter up into pieces – making sure they are cold. Whisk the whites until fluffy.
3. In another container, combine the baking powder and flour. Cut in the butter and add the salt. Fold in the mixture over the egg whites.

4. Drop the dough onto the baking pan or muffin tin.
5. Bake them for 12-15 minutes.

Cheddar Bay Biscuits

Servings Provided: (4) 8 biscuits – 2 per serving
Time Required: 50 minutes

Ingredients Needed:

- Cheddar cheese (1 cup)
- Cream cheese (4 oz.)
- Mozzarella cheese (1.5 cups)
- Large eggs (2)
- Almond flour (.66 cup)
- Granulated garlic powder (.5 tsp.)
- Baking powder (4 tsp.)
- Butter (as needed for the pan)

Preparation Technique:

1. Shred the mozzarella and cheddar cheese, and combine with the cream cheese to microwave for about 45 seconds using the high-power setting until melted. Stir and return for 20 additional seconds. Stir once more.
2. In another container, combine the eggs with the almond flour, garlic powder, and baking powder. Mix it all together and place it on a sheet of flour-dusted plastic wrap. Roll it up and put it into the fridge for 20-30 minutes.
3. Warm the oven at 425° Fahrenheit. Prepare a dark-colored baking dish with butter.
4. Slice the cold dough into eight segments. Place in the prepared pan – leaving a little space between each one.

5. Bake for 10-12 minutes. Take them out of the pan to cool.

Eggs Benedict

Servings Provided: 4
Time Required: 12 minutes

Ingredients Needed:

- Eggs (8)
- White wine vinegar (.25 cup)
- Hollandaise sauce (as desired)
- High-quality smoked ham (4 thick slices)
- English muffins (4)

Preparation Technique:

1. Warm the grill. Pour the water and vinegar into a saucepan.
2. Poach the eggs. After the water is gently boiling, gently break and slide the eggs into the water - as you avoid breaking the yolks. Set the timer for three minutes or until the whites are set with soft yolks.
3. Slice and toast both sides of the muffin.
4. Prepare them with a ham slice and let it warm while still on the grill.
5. Transfer the eggs to a towel-lined platter for a minute before preparing the sandwich.
6. Serve with the hollandaise sauce.

Fried Apples

Servings Provided: 10
Time Required: 30 minutes

Ingredients Needed:

- Butter (3 tbsp.)
- Golden Delicious apples (4 medium)
- Granulated sugar (.25 cup)
- Cinnamon (1 tsp.)
- Nutmeg (.25 tsp.)
- Packed brown sugar (2 tbsp.)
- Apple cider (.5 cup)
- Cornstarch (1 tbsp.)
- Also Needed: 12-inch skillet

Preparation Technique:

1. Core and slice the apples into about two pounds of ¾-inch wedges.
2. Prepare a skillet using the medium temperature setting to melt the butter.
3. Toss in the apples, spices, and sugar. Stir and place a lid on the pan.
4. Simmer for 11-14 minutes, occasionally stirring until tenderized.
5. Scoop into a serving dish to keep warm.
6. Whisk the cider and cornstarch together and pour into the skillet.
7. Simmer using medium heat for 30-60 seconds until it's thickened.
8. Pour the mixture over the apples before serving.

Lemon & Blueberry Ricotta Pancakes

Servings Provided: 12 - 1 dozen cakes
Time Required: 25 minutes

Ingredients Needed:

- Egg (1)
- Milk (1.75 cups)
- Ricotta cheese (.5 cup)
- Melted butter (2 tbsp.)
- Flour (1.5 cups)
- Salt (.5 tsp.)
- Sugar (2 tbsp.)
- Baking powder (3 tsp.)
- Vanilla (.5 tsp.)
- Fresh/frozen blueberries (1 cup)
- Lemon juice and zest (1 lemon)
- Milk (1 tbsp.)
- Powdered sugar (1 cup)

Preparation Technique:

1. Warm a cast iron pan or griddle using the medium temperature setting.
2. Whisk the egg, melted butter, milk, ricotta cheese, vanilla, and lemon zest.
3. Whisk the dry fixings (salt, baking powder, and flour) in another container. Slowly, add the combine the fixings to form a dough. Wait for about five minutes. Add more milk if it gets too 'puffy.'

4. Add butter to the grill and warm it using the med-low temperature setting.
5. Pour the mixture onto the griddle, adding a few blueberries over the top of each one.
6. Flip and cook until done. Keep the pancakes warm in the oven at 200° Fahrenheit as you prepare the rest of the cakes.
7. Whisk the milk, juice, and powdered sugar (warm if you choose) and serve over the pancakes.

Overnight Pumpkin Pie Oatmeal

Servings Provided: 2
Time Required: 5 minutes

Ingredients Needed:

- Pumpkin pie filling (.25 cup)
- Whole milk/your choice or Greek yogurt (.5 cup)
- Maple syrup (2 tsp.)
- Regular old-fashioned oats (.75 cup)
- Optional: Raisins (1 tbsp.)
- Shredded coconut (.25 cup)
- Chia seeds (1 tsp.)
- Protein powder (1 tbsp.)

Preparation Technique:

1. Whisk the whole milk, pie filling, and maple syrup in a mixing container until smooth and thoroughly combined (lump-free).
2. Stir the oats and other fixings into the pumpkin pie mixture.
3. Cover the bowl or individually pack the oatmeal in small mason jars with lids, and let them chill four hours or overnight to soften the oats.
4. After it has sat overnight, heat the oatmeal in the microwave or enjoy it cold! The oatmeal will stay tasty in the fridge for three to four days.

Potato Waffles

Servings Provided: 2
Time Required: 30 minutes

Ingredients Needed:

- Yellow potato (6-8 oz./1 large)
- Egg (1 beaten)
- A-P flour (1 tbsp.)
- Melted butter (1 tbsp.)
- Salt (.5 tsp.)
- Baking powder (.25 tsp.)
- Shredded cheese (.5 cup + more for topping)
- Bacon (.25 cup - cooked crumbled + more for topping)

   To Garnish:
- Crème fraîche
- Fresh chives

Preparation Technique:

1. Warm the waffle iron while you measure the fixings. Lightly grease the surface of the waffle iron as needed.
2. Shred the potato into a large bowl using a box grater. Squeeze the shredded potato to extract as much of the liquid as possible. As liquid releases, pour it off into a separate cup.
3. When finished, let the liquid in the bowl settle for a couple of minutes. A layer of starch will settle at the bottom of the bowl. Gently pour

the liquid off, retaining the starch beneath. Add this starch, adding it back into the shredded potato.
4. Whisk and mix in the egg, salt, butter, baking powder, and flour into the potato mixture. Combine and fold in the bacon and cheese.
5. With a large spoon, spread an even layer of batter onto the hot iron.
6. Cook until crisped and golden brown (5-7 min.).
7. Move the waffle to a plate and top with the creme fraiche, cheese, chives, and bacon. Serve promptly.

Sausage Egg & Cheese Breakfast Sliders

Servings Provided: 16
Time Required: 30 minutes

Ingredients Needed:

- Breakfast sausage - ex. Jimmy Dean (2 lb.)
- Eggs (8)
- Milk (.5 cup)
- Black pepper & salt (as desired)
- Colby Jack cheese (10 slices)
- Kings Hawaiian Rolls (16)

Preparation Technique:

1. Set the oven temperature at 350° Fahrenheit.
2. Whisk the eggs, salt, pepper, and milk.
3. Lightly spritz a casserole dish with cooking oil spray. Dump the egg mixture into the bowl.
4. Add the sausage into another baking dish, making an even layer.
5. Bake both of the dishes for about 15 to 20 minutes.
6. Slice the rolls and layer the sausage over the rolls, adding the egg, and cheese. Add the tops and pop them in the oven to melt the cheese.
7. Now, you are ready to slice and serve to enjoy the tasty sliders!

Scrambled Eggs With Cream Cheese

Servings Provided: 2
Time Required: 17 minutes

Ingredients Needed:

- Eggs (4 large)
- Cold full-fat cream cheese (2 oz.)
- Unsalted butter (2 tbsp.)
- Fresh chives (2 tsp.)
- Kosher salt and black pepper (as desired)

Preparation Technique:

1. Gather all of the fixings.
2. Break the four eggs into a large mixing container and vigorously mix them until foamy.
3. Chop the cream cheese into ½-inch cubes and mix it into the beaten eggs.
4. Warm a skillet using the high-temperature setting to melt the butter.
5. When the butter starts to foam, add the egg mixture.
6. When about ½ to ¾ of the egg has thickened into curds, remove the pan from the burner. Continue to shift the eggs around with the spatula.
7. Plate the eggs when thoroughly cooked to your liking.
8. Finely chop the chives and add them with a sprinkle of pepper and salt. Serve promptly.

Southern-Style Grits

Servings Provided: 4-6
Time Required: 35 minutes

Ingredients Needed:

- Water (4 cups)
- Stone-ground corn grits - ex. Anson Mills (1.5 cups)
- Bay leaves (2 dried)
- Kosher salt (.5 tsp.)
- Unsalted butter (1 stick/8 tbsp.)
- Parmesan cheese (2 oz.)
- Heavy cream (1 cup)

Preparation Technique:

1. Pour the water into a pot or dutch oven with the grits, bay leaves, and salt. Let the mixture come to boiling using the high-temperature setting. Once boiling, promptly transfer it to a cool burner, cover, and wait for about 15 minutes.
2. Uncover and boil the grits using the med-high heat setting. Continue cooking for 20-25 minutes.
3. When the water is mostly absorbed, take the pan from the burner and discard the bay leaves.
4. Mix in the butter, heavy cream, and cheese right before serving.

Sweet Potato Muffins With Cinnamon Sugar Topping

Servings Provided: 12
Time Required: 40 minutes

Ingredients Needed:

The Muffins:
- All-purpose flour (1.75 cups/8 oz.)
- Cinnamon (.75 tsp.)
- Baking powder (2.25 tsp.)
- Ground nutmeg (.5 tsp.)
- Salt (.5 tsp.)
- Granulated sugar (.25 cup)
- Large eggs (2)
- Packed light brown sugar (.25 cup)
- Evaporated/whole milk (.5 cup)
- Vanilla extract (.5 tsp.)
- Vegetable oil (.5 cup)
- Freshly cooked sweet potatoes or Sweet potato puréed from a can (1.33 cups)
- Chopped pecans (.5 cup)
- Optional: Toffee bits/brickle bits (.5 cup)

The Topping:
- Granulated sugar (2 tbsp.)
- Ground cinnamon (.5 tsp.)

Preparation Technique:

1. Heat the oven to 375° Fahrenheit.

2. Butter or spray the wells of a 12-cup muffin tin with cooking oil spray.
3. Sift the baking powder, flour, nutmeg, cinnamon, and salt.
4. Whisk the eggs with the brown sugar, vegetable oil, granulated sugar, evaporated milk, and vanilla extract. Lastly, mix in the potato purée and whisk it until it's thoroughly blended.
5. Fold the flour mixture into the potato batter - just until the dry mix is moistened. Fold in the pecans and toffee bits. Fill muffin cups nearly full.
6. Prepare the topping. Combine the granulated sugar with the cinnamon.
7. Sprinkle about ½ of a teaspoon of the cinnamon-sugar mixture over the muffins.
8. Bake the muffins for 22-26 minutes until nicely browned and serve.

Chapter 2: Poultry Favorites

Chicken & Dumplings

Servings Provided: 8
Time Required: 20 minutes

Ingredients Needed:

- Shredded cooked chicken meat (3 cups)
- Chicken broth (Three 14 oz. cans)
- Cream of chicken soup (Two 10.5 oz. cans)
- Refrigerated biscuit dough (Two 10 oz. cans)

Preparation Technique:

1. Stir the chicken broth, soup, and chicken in a Dutch oven using the med-high temperature setting.
2. Slice each biscuit into quarters. Once the soup is simmering, gently add the biscuits to the pot.
3. Adjust the temperature setting to med-low and cover.
4. Simmer to cook the biscuits until the dough is firm - not doughy (10-15 min.).

Crispy Oven-Fried Chicken

Servings Provided: 4
Time Required: 40 minutes + marinate time

Ingredients Needed:

- Chicken drumsticks (8)
- Non-fat buttermilk (4 cups)
- Salt (.25 cup)
- Chili powder (1 tsp.)
- Sugar (.25 cup)
- Hot sauce - ex. Frank's Red-Hot (1 tbsp.)
- Panko breadcrumbs (2 cups)
- Garlic salt (.5 tsp.)
- Vegetable/Canola oil (2 tbsp.)
- Also Needed: Rimmed baking sheet

Preparation Technique:

1. Measure and add the salt, hot sauce, buttermilk, sugar, and chicken in a zipper-type plastic bag. Toss the fixings and pop it into the fridge to marinate for a minimum of two hours. (You can let it rest for up to 12 hours or overnight.)
2. Warm the oven at 350° Fahrenheit. Adjust the rack to the center position.
3. Break the breadcrumbs into smaller pieces for the coating. Mix them in a container with the oil, chili powder, and garlic salt.
4. Remove the marinated chicken from the bag, allowing the excess liquid to drip away first.

Dredge each piece into the breadcrumbs until covered.
5. Arrange the pieces on the baking tray to bake for about half an hour, until the chicken is thoroughly cooked and the breadcrumbs are nicely browned.

Crockpot Orange Chicken

Servings Provided: 4-6
Time Required: 3-6 hours – varies

Ingredients Needed:

- Chicken breasts (3 lb.)
- Soy sauce (2 tbsp.)
- BBQ Sauce - ex. Sweet Baby Ray's® Original (.75 cup)
- Smuckers® Sweet Orange Marmalade (.75 cup)

Preparation Technique:

1. Thaw the chicken if frozen, removing all skin and bones. Toss it into the crockpot. Securely close the lid.
2. Set the cooker for three hours using the high function or six hours on the low setting.
3. Drain the cooking juices from the crockpot.
4. Dice the chicken into cubes, and toss it back into the cooker.
5. Mix the barbecue sauce, soy sauce, and marmalade. Dump the mixture over the chicken and close the top. Set the cooker using the high setting for 30 more minutes.
6. Serve with a portion of delicious rice.

Honey-Garlic Chicken

Servings Provided: 4
Time Required: 15 minutes

Ingredients Needed:

- Olive/canola oil (2 tsp.)
- Chicken breasts (1.5 lb.)
- Black pepper & salt (to your liking)
- Honey (3 tbsp.)
- Soy sauce (3 tbsp.)
- Garlic (3 cloves)
- Optional: Red pepper flakes (.25 cup)

  Optional: To Serve:
- Sliced green onions
- Brown rice
- Sesame seeds
- Wedges of lime

Preparation Technique:

1. Warm a skillet using the med-high temperature setting and add the oil.
2. Clean the chicken removing all fat and bones, and cube it into ½-inch pieces - sprinkling with pepper and salt. Toss it into the pan and fry (3-4 min.).
3. Mince the garlic. Prepare the glaze by whisking the garlic, soy sauce (low-sodium preferred), red pepper flakes, and honey in a mixing container.

4. Toss the chicken with the sauce and cook until it's thoroughly cooked (5-6 min.).
5. Serve and enjoy it with a squeeze of lime and your favorite side dishes.

Mozzarella Stuffed Chicken Parm

Servings Provided: 4
Time Required: 1 hour 15 minutes

Ingredients Needed:

- Chicken breasts (1 lb.)
- Fresh mozzarella (8 oz.)
- Black pepper & kosher salt
- A-P flour (1 cup)
- Eggs (3)
- Oregano - dried (1 tsp.)
- Panko breadcrumbs (1 cup)
- Garlic powder (.5 tsp.)
- Parmesan - divided (.5 cup)
- For Frying: Olive oil
- Marinara (2 cups)
- Thinly sliced basil (.25 cup)
- Chopped parsley (2 tbsp.)

Preparation Technique:

1. Warm the oven at 425° Fahrenheit.
2. Use a sharp paring knife to remove the fat and bones from the chicken. Slice a pocket for the stuffing into each breast.
3. Stuff the pockets using mozzarella, pressing the edges of the chicken together to seal. Dust it using pepper and salt.
4. Prepare three shallow bowls.
5. Whisk the eggs in one.
6. Measure the flour and breadcrumbs. Prepare the breadcrumbs by mixing with the ½

teaspoon of salt, garlic powder, oregano, and ¼ cup freshly grated parmesan.
7. Dip the stuffed chicken in each of the bowls;
    a. Flour - shaking off excess
    b. Egg - dip the chicken - tossing to coat.
    c. Breadcrumbs - evenly coated.
8. Prepare a large skillet using the medium temperature setting, and pour in a thin layer of oil.
9. Cook the stuffed chicken for about four minutes on each side.
10. Dump and stir in the marinara and basil. Extinguish the heat and sprinkle the rest of the parmesan over the chicken.
11. Transfer the skillet into the heated oven to bake for about 20 minutes.
12. Serve hot with a sprinkle of fresh parsley.

Quick & Easy Air Fryer Chicken Breast

Servings Provided: 2
Time Required: 30 minutes

Ingredients Needed:

- Egg (1 large)
- All-purpose flour (.25 cup)
- Panko breadcrumbs (.75 cup)
- Freshly grated parmesan (.33 cup)
- Lemon zest (2 tsp.)
- Cayenne pepper (.5 tsp.)
- Oregano - dried (1 tsp.)
- Black pepper and kosher salt
- Chicken breasts (2)

Preparation Technique:

1. Whisk the eggs in a shallow dish. In another bowl, add the flour. In a third shallow bowl, mix the oregano, parmesan, panko, lemon zest, salt, pepper, and cayenne.
2. Discard the bones and fat from the chicken. Dredge the chicken into flour, eggs, and panko mixture - tossing in each to thoroughly cover.
3. Individually, arrange the coated chicken in the Air Fryer basket.
4. Let the Air Fryer heat at 375° Fahrenheit and cook them for ten minutes.
5. Trim the chicken and continue to air-fry until the coating is crispy (5 min.).

Roasted Chicken With Pan Gravy

Servings Provided: 4-6
Time Required: 2 hours

Ingredients Needed:

- Naturally-raised chicken (3 lb.)
- Rosemary (2 sprigs)
- Thyme (2 sprigs)
- Garlic (2 cloves)
- Parsley (1 sprig)
- Softened butter - divided (3 tbsp.)
- Paprika (1 tsp.)
- Sea salt
- Medium onion (1 quartered)
- All-purpose flour (1 tbsp.)
- Homemade/good-quality purchased chicken stock (2 cups)

Preparation Technique:

1. Warm the oven at 400° Fahrenheit.
2. Thoroughly rinse and dry the chicken with several paper towels.
3. Tie the thyme, rosemary, and parsley together with a 100% cotton kitchen string and toss it and the garlic inside the bird cavity.
4. Rub the outside with two tablespoons of the butter and sprinkle with paprika and salt. Put the chicken on a roasting rack in a roasting pan. Place the onion quarters on the rack under the chicken.

5. Wait for the chicken to reach room temperature before placing it on the center rack of the oven. Set a timer and roast it for 15 minutes.
6. Adjust the temperature of the oven to 350° Fahrenheit and roast until it's well done or has an internal temp of 170° Fahrenheit (75 to 90 min.).
7. Transfer the chicken from the rack and let it rest on a platter.
8. Prepare the gravy. Drain the juices from the roasting pan into a measuring cup and skim off the fat for another use. Add the rest of the juices to your stock. Leave the onion in a roasting pan.
9. Combine flour and the remaining one tablespoon of butter. Add that mixture to the roasting pan.
10. Put the skillet on the stovetop using the med-high temperature setting.
11. Swirl the butter and flour mixture for a minute or two or until melted and bubbly. Pour in ½ cup of the stock mixture to the roasting pan, scraping gently with a wooden spatula to deglaze the pan. Pour the liquid and solids into a saucepan, including the salt, pepper, and remaining stock mixture.
12. Boil it using the medium temperature setting.
13. Simmer the gravy for 10 to 20 minutes to reduce to sauce consistency. Serve it with carved chicken.

Chapter 3: Ground Beef Favorites

American Beef Goulash

Servings Provided: 6
Time Required: 40 minutes

Ingredients Needed:

- Dry elbow macaroni (1.5 cups)
- Ground chuck (1.5 lb.)
- Onion (1 medium)
- Garlic cloves (2 medium)
- Italian seasoning (1 tsp.)
- Seasoning salt - ex. Lawry's (1 tsp.)
- Black pepper, freshly cracked (.5 tsp.)
- Optional: Cajun seasoning- ex. Slap Ya Mama (.25-.5 tsp.)
- Bay leaves (2 small)
- Tomato sauce (8-oz. can)
- Optional: Granulated sugar (1 pinch)
- Undrained diced tomatoes (2 cans each @ 14.5-oz.)
- Optional: Red pepper flakes

Preparation Technique:

1. Chop the onion and mince the cloves.
2. Prepare the macaroni until it is al dente (reserving two cups of the pasta water). Dump the macaroni into a colander to drain.

3. Sauté the beef uncovered, draining the cooking fat. Toss in the onion and garlic to sauté for five to six minutes.
4. Mix in the Italian seasoning, seasoned salt, pepper, bay leaves, and Cajun seasoning.
5. Pour in the undrained diced tomatoes, sugar, and tomato sauce - scraping up the tasty browned bits.
6. Once the mixture is boiling, adjust the temperature setting and cover. Simmer it for 15 minutes, occasionally stirring.
7. Dump the macaroni and reserved pasta water as needed to loosen the mixture. Continue simmering until the pasta is thoroughly warmed. Sprinkle with red pepper flakes as desired.
8. Remove the pan to a cool burner and discard the bay leaves.
9. Serve promptly.
10. For a cheesy variation, cube about ½ cup of Velveeta and stir in just before serving, until it's melted and creamy.

Barbeque Burgers

Servings Provided: 6
Time Required: 40 minutes

Ingredients Needed:

The Sauce:
- Packed brown sugar (.5 cup)
- Ketchup (1 cup)
- Worcestershire sauce (1.5 tsp.)
- Sugar (1/3 cup)
- Molasses (.25 cup)
- Honey (.25 cup)
- Prepared mustard (2 tsp.)
- Pepper (1/8 tsp.)
- Salt (.25 tsp.)
- Liquid smoke (.25 tsp.)

The Burgers:
- Whisked egg (1 large)
- Quick-cooking oats (1/3 cup)
- Onion salt (.25 tsp.)
- Pepper (.25 tsp.)
- Garlic salt (.25 tsp.)
- Salt (1/8 tsp.)
- Ground beef (1.5 lb.)
- Split burger buns (6)

Preparation Technique:

1. Warm a small saucepan and combine the first ten sauce fixings. Once boiling, transfer to a

cool burner. Set aside one cup of the sauce to serve with the burgers.
2. Whisk the egg and mix with the oats, onion salt, garlic salt, pepper, salt, and ¼ cup of the bbq sauce. Mix in the beef and shape it into six patties.
3. Grill with the lid on using the medium temperature setting to reach an internal temp of 160° Fahrenheit (6-8 min. per side).
4. Baste it using ½ cup of the sauce during the last five minutes of the grilling cycle.
5. Serve on buns using the reserved barbecue sauce and garnishes to your liking.

Cheesy Fiesta Beef Casserole - Texas-Style

Servings Provided: 8
Time Required: 40 minutes

Ingredients Needed:

- Ground beef (1 lb.)
- Onion (1 medium)
- Black beans (15 oz. can)
- Picante sauce (1 cup)
- Chili powder (.5 tsp.)
- Undiluted condensed cream of chicken soup (10.5 oz. can)
- Undrained tomatoes & green chiles - diced (10 oz. can)
- Green chiles (4 oz. can)
- Tortilla chips - crushed - ex. Nacho-flavored/plain (9.75 oz. pkg.)
- Shredded sharp & Monterey Jack cheese (1 cup of each)
- Also Needed: Lightly greased 2.5-quart baking dish

Preparation Technique:

1. Chop the onion and green chiles. Rinse and drain the beans.
2. Prepare a skillet using the medium temperature setting for cooking the onion and beef and onion until well done (6-8 min.), breaking the meat into crumbles, and drain.

Stir in the beans, Picante sauce, and chili powder.
3. Combine the soup, tomatoes, and green chiles in a mixing container.
4. Layer about half of the chips, the beef mix, soup mixture, and cheeses. Continue the layering until all fixings are used.
5. Microwave using the med-high function, uncovered until it's heated thoroughly, and the cheese is melted (12 min.).
6. Serve with a portion of avocado and sour cream.

Chipotle Chili Sloppy Joes

Servings Provided: 6
Time Required: 35 minutes

Ingredients Needed:

- Lean ground beef (1 lb.)
- Sweet onion (1 cup)
- Green pepper (.5 cup)
- Optional: Jalapeno pepper - seeded (1)
- Chili sauce (.5 cup)
- Water (.5 cup)
- Chipotle peppers in the adobo sauce (1-2)
- Yellow mustard (1 tsp.)
- Packed brown sugar (1 tbsp.)
- Split burger buns or kaiser rolls (6)
- Softened butter (2 tbsp.)
- Optional: Sliced pickles

Preparation Technique:

1. Finely chop the onion, pepper, and jalapeno, and chipotle peppers.
2. Warm the oven broiler.
3. Prepare a large cast-iron skillet using the medium heat temperature setting to sauté the green pepper, onion, and jalapeno, and (5-7 min.).
4. Drain the fixings and stir in the chili sauce, brown sugar, and mustard, water, and chipotle peppers; bring the fixings to a boil. Simmer, uncovered (8-10 min.) stirring occasionally.

5. Lightly butter the cut sides of rolls and arrange them on a baking tray with the buttered side upward. Broil them three to four inches from the heat until lightly toasted (30 sec.). Fill with beef mixture and pickles.

Cincinnati Chili

Servings Provided: 4
Time Required: 40 minutes

Ingredients Needed:

- Multigrain spaghetti (12 oz.)
- Vegetable oil (2 tsp.)
- Ground beef sirloin (12 oz.)
- Onion (1 small)
- Garlic (2 cloves)
- Chili powder (2 tbsp.)
- Unsweetened cocoa (1 tbsp.)
- Black pepper and salt (.25 tsp. each)
- Brown sugar (1 tbsp.)
- Cinnamon (1 tsp.)
- Ground cumin (.5 tsp.)
- No-salt-added crushed tomatoes (28 oz. can/as desired)
- Kidney beans (15.5 oz. can)
- Cheddar cheese (1 cup)
- Green onions (3)

Preparation Technique:

1. Cover a pot of salted water - setting the temperature on the high setting. Cook the spaghetti as the label directs.
2. Warm oil in a three-quart saucepan using the med-high temperature setting.
3. Cook the garlic, onion, and beef for two minutes, stirring and breaking up meat with a wooden spoon.

4. Add cinnamon, cumin, chili powder, cocoa, sugar, pepper, and salt. Cook for one minute while stirring. Add in the tomatoes.
5. Simmer for eight minutes or until slightly thickened. Mix in the beans to simmer for two minutes or until the beans are heated thoroughly.
6. Drain the spaghetti and portion it among four serving plates. Top with chili, cheese, and green onions.

Family Meatloaf

Servings Provided: 16
Time Required: 1 hour 15 minutes

Ingredients Needed:

- Light brown sugar (.25 cup)
- Low-sodium soy sauce (4 tsp.)
- Ketchup (1.25 cups)
- Worcestershire sauce (.25 cup)
- Fresh bread (2 cups)
- Whole milk (.5 cup)
- Celery (.5 cup)
- Onion (1 cup)
- Garlic (1 tbsp.)
- Parsley (.25 cup)
- Dry mustard (1 tbsp.)
- Coarse black pepper (1 tsp.)
- Fresh thyme (2 tsp.)
- Large eggs (3)
- Kosher salt (2 tsp.)
- Ground Meat:
    - Beef (1.5 lb.)
    - Pork (1 lb.)
    - Veal (.5 lb.)
- Onion (1 medium)
- Thyme (8 sprigs)
- Bacon (6 slices)
- Also Needed: Loaf pan - 16x5-inch

Preparation Technique:

1. Prepare a baking tray using a layer of parchment baking paper. Lightly grease a loaf pan.
2. Whisk the ketchup, brown sugar, Worcestershire sauce, and soy sauce in a mixing container. Set aside.
3. Warm the oven at 400° Fahrenheit. Add the milk and bread in a container and let sit for five minutes.
4. Mince and combine the garlic, celery, onion, eggs, parsley, mustard, thyme, pepper, and salt in a mixing container. Mix in the bread, meat, and 1/3 cup of the ketchup glaze.
5. Transfer the meat mixture into the prepared pan and cover using 1/3 cup of the ketchup glaze.
6. Toss the onion rings with two tablespoons of the ketchup glaze and spread them over the top of the meatloaf. Toss the sprigs of thyme over the onions and twist the bacon over the loaf.
7. Arrange the pan on the center oven rack on a baking tray to avoid spills and bake for 15 minutes.
8. Adjust the oven temperature setting to 350° Fahrenheit and bake until an internal temperature of 160° Fahrenheit is reached (50 min.).
9. Transfer the pan to the countertop to rest. Serve after 15 minutes with the remainder of the delicious glaze.

Glazed Bacon & Cheese Burgers

Servings Provided: 4
Time Required: 20 minutes

Ingredients Needed:

- Dark brown sugar (3 tbsp.)
- Garlic powder (.5 tsp.)
- Paprika (1.5 tsp.)
- Ground cumin (.5 tsp.)
- Chipotle powder (.25 tsp.)
- Salt (.25 tsp.)
- Freshly cracked black pepper (.25 tsp.)
- Ground beef (1 lb.)
- Shredded sharp cheddar cheese (.5 cup)
- Bacon (6 slices)
- Rolls (4)

Preparation Technique:

1. Warm the grill using the medium temperature setting. Whisk the pepper, salt, spices, and sugar and set aside.
2. Shape the beef into eight patties.
3. Toss the cheese and cooked-crumbled bacon and sprinkle over four of the burgers.
4. Add the other four patties to the top, pinching it all into one burger.
5. Cover each of the burgers with the spice mixture and grill about five minutes on each side (for medium).
6. Serve with your favorite side dishes or right off of the grill.

One-Skillet Shepherd's Beef Pie

Servings Provided: 8-10
Time Required: 55 minutes

Ingredients Needed:

- Olive oil (3 tbsp.)
- Ground beef (2 lb. lean)
- Unsalted butter (3 tbsp.)
- Yellow onion (1 large)
- Carrots (2-3)
- Baby portobello/cremini mushrooms (12-16 oz.)
- Garlic (4 cloves)
- Kosher salt - divided (1 tbsp.)
- Dried oregano (1.5 tsp.)
- Tomato paste (3-6 tbsp./as desired)
- Beef stock (.5-1 cup)
- Worcestershire sauce (1 tsp.)
- Black pepper (.5 tsp./as desired)
- Mashed potatoes (3-4 cups)
- Shredded parmesan cheese (1/3 cup)
- Butter (1.5 tbsp.)
- The Garnish: Fresh parsley

Preparation Technique:

1. Peel and dice the onions and carrots. Rinse and quarter the mushrooms. Mince the garlic and parsley.
2. Warm the oven at 375° Fahrenheit.
3. Use the medium temperature setting to warm a cast-iron skillet. Pour in the oil and beef to

simmer for four minutes - breaking it into chunks while it's cooking. Drain the grease and drain on a layer of paper towels in a mixing container.
4. Add butter to the pan to melt. Add the prepared carrots, onion, garlic, mushrooms, half of the salt, and oregano. Simmer it for eight to ten minutes - stirring intermittently.
5. Add the tomato paste and stir while cooking for five to seven minutes.
6. Add the beef back in the pan with the Worcestershire sauce, beef stock, pepper, and rest of the salt. Simmer it for several minutes until it's thickened.
7. Top with a layer of mashed potatoes and parmesan.
8. Rough-up the potatoes and dot with cubes of butter.
9. Bake for 40 to 45 minutes. Wait for about five to ten minutes to serve with a portion of freshly minced parsley.

Texas Beef Tacos

Servings Provided: 10
Time Required: 30 minutes

Ingredients Needed:

- Lean ground beef (1.5 lb.)
- Onion (1 small)
- Sweet red pepper (1 medium)
- Tomato sauce (8 oz. can)
- Diced tomatoes (14.5 oz. can)
- Frozen corn (1.33 cups)
- Chili powder (2 tbsp.)
- Salt (.5 tsp.)
- Ready-to-serve brown rice (8.8 oz. pkg.)
- Taco shells (20 warmed)

Preparation Technique:

1. Chop the onion and bell pepper. Drain the tomatoes and thaw the corn.
2. Prepare a Dutch oven using the medium temperature setting. Mix in the red pepper, onions, and beef to simmer until all are done (8-10 min.). Drain the fat.
3. Stir in the salt, chili powder, tomato sauce, corn, and tomatoes.
4. Once the mixture starts to boil, add the rice and heat it thoroughly.
5. Serve on the shells with the toppings you prefer, such as lettuce, tomatoes, or a portion of reduced-fat sour cream.

Worcestershire-Glazed Burgers

Servings Provided: 8
Time Required: 35 minutes

Ingredients Needed:

- Ground beef (2.5 lb.)
- Black pepper & kosher salt (as desired)
- Worcestershire sauce (3 tbsp.)
- Burger buns (8)
- Canola oil (as needed)

    To Serve:

- Lettuce
- Sliced tomatoes
- Pickles
- Cheese

Preparation Technique:

1. Set up the grill using the med-high. Clean and lightly oil grates with oil before you start cooking.
2. Shape the beef into eight ¾-inch patties, dusting with pepper and salt.
3. Make a slight indentation in each patty and grill until they are easily lifted from the grates (3-4 min.).
4. Flip and grill the second side, basting with Worcestershire for about four minutes for medium doneness.
5. Prepare the glazed burgers and serve on buns with the toppings to your liking.

Chapter 4: Favorite Beef Cuts

Beef Stroganoff

Servings Provided: 4
Time Required: 35 minutes

Ingredients Needed:

- Onion (.5 cup)
- Boneless beef round steak (.5 lb.)
- Uncooked yolkless egg noodles (4 cups)
- All-purpose flour (1 tbsp.)
- Water (.5 cup)
- Undiluted - cream of mushroom soup (half of a small can)
- Paprika (.5 tsp.)
- Fat-free sour cream (.5 cup)

Preparation Technique:

1. Discard the fat from the steak and slice it into ¾-inch thick pieces.
2. Warm a skillet using the medium-temperature heat setting. Chop and mix in the onions to sauté for about five minutes. Toss the beef in the pan to cook five additional five minutes. Drain and set it to the side.
3. Boil a large saucepan or Dutch oven about ¾ full of water. When boiling, stir in the noodles to cook for about 10-12 minutes. Drain the pasta thoroughly.

4. In another saucepan, mix the water, soup, and flour using the medium heat setting. Mix in the paprika.
5. Combine the two until thoroughly warmed. Place the pan on a cool burner and mix in the sour cream.
6. Stir and serve.

Chicken-Fried Steak

Servings Provided: 4
Time Required: 45 minutes

Ingredients Needed:

- Steak (1 lb.)
- A-P flour (2 cups)
- Paprika (1 tbsp.)
- Cayenne pepper (1 tsp.)
- Buttermilk/alternative: Eggs (2 cups)
- Black pepper & salt
- Neutral oil (a few cups/as needed for frying)

The Gravy:

- Flour (4 tbsp.)
- Butter (2 tbsp.)
- Oil from Frying (2 tbsp.)
- Milk (2 cups)
- Black pepper and salt (to your liking)

Preparation Technique:

1. Slice the steaks into a ¼ inch thickness and pound out with a tenderizer. Dust the using a portion of pepper and salt.
2. Dump the flour into a large mixing container and add seasonings.
3. Toss the steak cuts into the buttermilk/whisked eggs. Dredge them through the flour mix. Set the meat aside.
4. Pour oil into a skillet using the med-high temperature setting. After the pan is heated,

add enough oil to come up about halfway on the steaks.
5. Toss the steak cuts into the oil and fry for four minutes on each side. You can work them in batches, so they're not touching.
6. Transfer the steaks onto a platter lined with paper towels to drain.
7. Discard all the oil in the pan except about two tablespoons and leave all the browned bits.
8. Toss the butter into the skillet to help remove the bits of steak from the bottom. Adjust the temperature to the low setting.
9. Sprinkle in flour and whisk to make a roux. Simmer approximately a minute until roux is browned.
10. Slowly whisk in the milk - about ½ of a cup at a time - whisking until the lumps are removed. Pour in the milk and a generous amount of pepper and salt (as desired), and simmer until thickened.
11. Serve the delicious country-style steaks with gravy and sides such as potatoes, a salad, or biscuits.

Crockpot Pepper Steak

Servings Provided: 4-6
Time Required: 8 hours (cook time) +20 minutes

Ingredients Needed:

- Beef stew meat (16 oz.)
- Bell peppers (2)
- Vegetable oil (1 tbsp./as needed)
- Worcestershire sauce (3 tbsp.)
- Garlic (1 tsp.)
- Stewed tomatoes (1 large can/as desired)
- Beef broth (1 can)
- Season salt (1 tsp./to taste)
- A-P flour (1-2 tbsp./as needed)

Preparation Technique:

1. Whisk the flour and season salt then coat the meat in the mixture.
2. Warm the oil in a skillet and add in the minced garlic, meat, bell peppers (in strips). Sauté them until the meat begins browning.
3. Transfer the mixture from the skillet to the slow cooker leaving the grease behind.
4. In the same skillet, pour in the stewed tomatoes with juice and one can of beef broth.
5. Slowly mix in the flour - while stirring until you make a gravy. Dump it over the meat in the slow cooker.
6. Securely close the lid and set the timer for eight hours using the low-temperature setting.

Philly Cheesesteak Sliders

Servings Provided: 12 sliders
Time Required: 45 minutes

Ingredients Needed:

- Olive oil (1 tbsp.)
- Green pepper (1 large)
- Onion (1 large)
- Freshly shaved steak (.5 lb.)
- Worcestershire sauce (1 tbsp.)
- Ground garlic powder (.5 tsp.)
- Pepper & salt (to your liking)
- Sweet-bread buns(12-pack)
- Provolone cheese (6 slices)
- Melted butter (1 tbsp.)
- Dried thyme - not ground (1 tsp.)
- Worcestershire sauce (.5 tsp.)

Preparation Technique:

1. Set the oven temperature at 400° Fahrenheit.
2. Prepare a skillet to warm the oil. Slice and toss in the onions and green peppers. Sauté them using the med-high temperature setting - occasionally stirring until the peppers and onions have softened.
3. Add the shaved steak, garlic powder, salt, pepper, and Worcestershire sauce. Break the steak apart using two forks to prevent the steak from clumping. Cook until the steak is no longer red and set it aside.

4. Slice the rolls in half horizontally, while keeping the 12-pack of buns intact. Arrange it onto a baking tray. Spread the steak mixture over the buns with a slice of cheese and the top half of the buns.
5. Melt and whisk the butter and mix it with the dried thyme and Worcestershire sauce. Brush the butter mixture generously over the top of the buns.
6. Place the sliders into the heated oven to bake until the cheese has melted (17-20 min.). Serve when they are as you like them.

Cheesesteak Quesadillas

Servings Provided: 8 portions
Time Required: 40 minutes

Ingredients Needed:

- Beef top sirloin (1 lb.)
- Onions (2 small)
- Green bell peppers (2)
- Barbeque sauce (ex. - Bull's-Eye Texas-Style Bold (1 cup)
- Flour tortillas (8-10 inches)
- Shredded cheddar cheese (2 cups)

Preparation Technique:

1. Set the oven at 425° Fahrenheit.
2. Warm a skillet using the medium-temperature setting. Thinly slice and add the beef to simmer until browned (5 to 7 min.).
3. Slice and toss in the peppers and onions. Simmer, stirring until softened (5-10 min.). Pour barbeque sauce over beef mixture and simmer until the sauce is slightly reduced (10 min.)
4. Lay 4 tortillas on a baking tray and prepare with the beef mix and cheese. Top each cheese layer with a tortilla.
5. Bake in the hot oven for ten minutes; flip the quesadillas and continue cooking until the cheese is melted (5 additional minutes).

Chapter 5: Seafood Favorites

Air Fryer Cod

Servings Provided: 2
Time Required: 20 minutes

Ingredients Needed:

- Cod (1 lb. cod)
- Kosher salt
- Black pepper & kosher salt (to taste)
- A-P flour (.5 cup)
- Egg (1 large)
- Panko breadcrumbs (2 cups)
- Old Bay seasoning (1 tsp.)

    To Serve:

- Tartar sauce
- Lemon wedges

Preparation Technique:

1. Pat fish dry and slice it into four strips. Dust both sides with salt and pepper.
2. Portion the flour, egg, and breadcrumbs with Old Bay into three shallow bowls.
3. Working one at a time, coat the fish in flour, egg, and lastly in the panko mix, pressing to coat.
4. Working in batches, place the fish in the basket of the Air Fryer and cook at 400° Fahrenheit

for 10-12 minutes, gently flipping halfway through the cooking cycle.
5. Serve with lemon wedges and tartar sauce.

Baked Catfish

Servings Provided: 4
Time Required: 30 minutes

Ingredients Needed:

- Olive oil - divided (.25 cup)
- Cornmeal (1 cup)
- Cajun seasoning (1 tbsp.)
- Catfish (4 fillets)
- Kosher salt and pepper
- Lemon wedges as desired

Preparation Technique:

1. Warm the oven at 425° Fahrenheit and drizzle two tablespoons of oil over a large baking sheet.
2. On a large plate, combine the Cajun seasoning, salt, pepper, and cornmeal.
3. Dredge the fish through the cornmeal, pressing to coat.
4. Place fish on the prepared baking tray and drizzle with the remaining two tablespoons of oil.
5. Bake until the fish is easily flaked using a fork (15 min.). Portion onto the plates and serve with a side of lemon wedges.

Best Tuna Melt

Servings Provided: 4
Time Required: 45 minutes

Ingredients Needed:

- Mayonnaise (.33 cup)
- Juice of ½ lemon
- Optional: Crushed red pepper flakes (.5 tsp.)
- Tuna (2 - 6-oz. cans)
- Celery (1 rib)
- Dill pickles (2)
- Red onion (.25 cup)
- Freshly chopped parsley (2 tbsp.)
- Black pepper and salt (to taste)
- Sourdough bread (9 slices)
- Butter (2 tbsp.)
- Tomato (1 sliced)
- Cheddar (8 slices)

Preparation Technique:

1. Set the oven at 400° Fahrenheit.
2. Whisk the mayo, lemon juice, and red pepper flakes.
3. Drain the tuna and mix it with the mayonnaise mixture.
4. Flake the tuna with a fork and finely chop. Add the celery, pickles, red onion, salt, pepper, and parsley, tossing to combine.
5. Butter one side of each bread slice. Top an unbuttered side with approximately ½ of a cup of tuna salad, two to three slices of tomato, and

two slices of cheese. Top with another slice of bread, buttered side facing up.
6. Continue with the rest of the ingredients and place them on a large baking tray.
7. Bake the sandwich until the cheese is melted (5-8 min.).

Blackened Catfish Sandwich With Cabbage & Avocado

Servings Provided: 4
Time Required: 15 minutes

Ingredients Needed:

- Plain Greek-style yogurt (1 cup)
- Sriracha (1 tsp.)
- Juice of one lime
- Canola oil (1 tbsp.)
- Catfish or Tilapia fillets (4 @ 6 oz. each)
- Blackening seasoning (1 tbsp.)
- Whole-wheat sesame seed buns (4)
- Avocado (1)
- Shredded red cabbage (2 cups)
- Pickled onions

Preparation Technique:

1. Combine the yogurt, lime juice, and sriracha. Set the mixture to the side for now.
2. Warm the oil in a cast-iron skillet using the high-temperature setting.
3. Rub the fish fillets on both sides with plenty of blackening seasoning.
4. Once the oil in the pan is smoking, add the fish and cook, undisturbed until a dark crust forms (3 min.).
5. Flip the fillets and cook until the fish flakes with gentle pressure from your finger (2-3 min.).

6. Meanwhile, toast the buns (cut side up) under the broiler.
7. Peel, slice, and portion the avocado and cabbage among the buns. Top with the hot fish, yogurt sauce, and onions.

Connecticut-Style Lobster Roll

Servings Provided: 4
Time Required: 45 minutes

Ingredients Needed:

- Lobster tails, steamed, meat removed and chopped (3 - 12-oz./3 cups)
- Butter (.25 cup - divided)
- Split-top hot dog buns (4)
- Freshly chopped chives (2 tbsp.)
- Kosher salt
- Black pepper
- Lemon wedges - as desired to serve

Preparation Technique:

1. Melt two tablespoons of butter and brush over the cut sides of hot dog buns. Warm a large skillet using the medium temperature setting and add the buns - cut side down. (It is easier to work in batches.) Toast the buns until browned as desired (1-2 min.).
2. Take them from the pan and add the remainder of the butter. Adjust the temperature setting to low.
3. Add the lobster in with the melted butter and simmer until it is warmed thoroughly (3-4 min.). Sprinkle the lobster with pepper and salt.
4. Fill the toasted buns with lobster a sprinkle of chopped chives. Serve with lemon wedges for an extra burst of flavor.

East Coast Shrimp & Lentil Bowls

Servings Provided: 4
Time Required: 35 minutes

Ingredients Needed:

- Dried brown lentils (.5 cup)
- Olive oil (1 tbsp.)
- Salt (.125 tsp.)
- Water (1.75 cups)
- Garlic powder - divided (2 tbsp.)
- Raw shrimp (26-30 count/1 lb.)
- Seafood seasoning (2 tsp.)
- Butter (2 tbsp.)
- Crushed red pepper flakes (.5 tsp.)
- Lemon juice (2 tsp.)
- Fresh baby spinach (3 cups)
- Ground nutmeg (.25 tsp.)
- Sweet onion (.25 cup)
- Lemon wedges

Preparation Technique:

1. Rinse the spinach in a colander and set it aside to drain.
2. Rinse the lentils and add them with the oil, salt, water, and one tablespoon garlic powder in a small saucepan. Once it's boiling, adjust the temperature setting to simmer, covered, until the lentils are tender (17-20 min.).
3. Peel, devein, and toss the shrimp with seafood seasoning.

4. Prepare a large skillet to melt the butter using the med-high temperature setting. Add pepper flakes and remaining garlic powder and stir for about half a minute.
5. Fold in the shrimp and simmer, stirring until the shrimp turn pink (3-4 min). Stir in lemon juice and remove the shrimp from the pan, keeping them warm.
6. Add the spinach and nutmeg to the pan and simmer using the med-high temperature setting until the spinach wilts. Remove it from heat.
7. Divide the lentils into four bowls, adding the shrimp, spinach, and finely chopped onion. Serve with lemon wedges.

Garlic Parmesan Flounder

Servings Provided: 4
Time Required: 35 minutes

Ingredients Needed:

- Olive oil (.25 cup)
- Flounder (4 fillets)
- Salt & pepper (to your liking)
- Parmesan cheese - freshly grated (.5 cup)
- Breadcrumbs (.25 cup)
- Garlic (4 cloves)
- Juice and zest of 1 lemon

Preparation Technique:

1. Set the oven at 425° Fahrenheit. Drizzle two tablespoons of oil over a large baking tray.
2. Sprinkle the flounder using the pepper and salt.
3. On a large platter, combine the parmesan, breadcrumbs, minced garlic, and lemon zest.
4. Dredge fish in breadcrumb mixture, pressing to coat.
5. Arrange the fish onto the greased baking tray and drizzle with the remaining two tablespoons oil and lemon juice.
6. Bake until the fish are golden and flaky (20 min.).

Lemon Pan-Fried Trout

Servings Provided: 2
Time Required: 25 minutes

Ingredients Needed:

- Trout (1 whole large/1 lb.)
- Baking & pancake mix (1 plate)
- Freshly cracked black pepper & salt
- Lemon pepper
- Triple Oil Blend (2-3 tbsp./see below)
- Lemon zest - grated

  The Oil Blend - 1/3 tbsp. each:
- Virgin cold-pressed coconut oil - melted
- Olive oil - extra-virgin (high-quality)
- Unrefined sesame oil

Preparation Technique:

1. Rinse the fish using cold water and dry with paper towels. Slash the fish diagonal along both sides.
2. Whisk the pepper and salt with the baking mix to cover the fish.
3. Warm the triple oil in a large skillet until bubbling. Add and cook the trout for about five minutes per side until golden brown and flakes easily with a fork.
4. Sprinkle with some lemon zest and serve.
5. *Notes*: You can prepare the fish with the head off or on, but you need to remove the gills. Either serve whole or fillet before serving.

Maple Bacon Salmon

Servings Provided: 6
Time Required: 50 minutes

Ingredients Needed:

The Salmon:
- Lemon (1 - wedges & juiced - 2 tbsp.)
- Skin-on salmon fillet (2.25 lb.)
- Himalayan Pink Salt - garlic - all-purpose seasoning - black pepper (2 1/2 tsp. - divided)
- Olive oil (.33 cup)
- Maple syrup (2 tbsp.)
- Dijon mustard (1 tbsp.)
- To Garnish: Diced chives

The Candied Bacon:

- Packed brown sugar (1 tbsp.)
- Himalayan Pink Salt (.25 tsp./as desired)
- Black pepper
- Garlic all-purpose seasoning
- Maple syrup (3 tbsp.)
- Bacon (6 slices)
- Also Needed: 9x13-inch baking dish

Preparation Technique:

1. Set the oven temperature at 400° Fahrenheit. Arrange lemon slices and salmon in a baking dish with two teaspoons of the pink salt, pepper, and garlic seasoning.
2. Whisk the mustard, oil, maple syrup, lemon juice, and remaining ½ of a teaspoon pink salt,

seasoning, and pepper. Pour the sauce over the fish.
3. Roast the salmon until it easily flakes with a fork (20-25 min.). Adjust the oven setting to broil. Add the salmon and roast until it's golden (3 min.).
4. Make the candied bacon. Whisk the maple syrup with pepper, ¼ teaspoon of pink salt, brown sugar, and garlic seasoning.
5. Warm a skillet using the medium temperature setting. Fry the bacon until it's lightly golden on both sides (4 min. on each side), draining off the fat.
6. Crumble the bacon and return it to the skillet and add the maple syrup mixture, turning the slices often until the bacon is glazed (3-4 min.).
7. Transfer the bacon to a baking tray to cool.
8. Garnish the salmon with the bacon bits and chives to serve.

Old-Fashioned Salmon Patties

Servings Provided: 10 patties
Time Required: 15 minutes

Ingredients Needed:

- Pink salmon (6 oz. can)
- Onion (2 tbsp.)
- Salt and pepper (to your liking)
- Large egg (1)
- Buttermilk (1 tbsp.)
- Cornmeal (2 tbsp.)
- A-P flour (4 tbsp.)
- For Frying: Vegetable oil (as needed)

Preparation Technique:

1. Drain the salmon - removing all skin and bones.
2. Dice the onion and mix with the salt, pepper, and salmon. Stir in the buttermilk, egg, flour, and cornmeal, mixing thoroughly.
3. Warm a cast-iron skillet and warm about ¼-inch of oil using the med-high temperature setting.
4. Drop the salmon mix by spoonfuls into the hot oil and slightly flatten.
5. Prepare the salmon in batches if needed, cooking about one minute on each side. Place them onto a towel-lined platter to remove the excess grease.
6. Serve any way desired with a side or as a sandwich.

Oysters Rockefeller

Servings Provided: 24
Time Required: 1 hour 35 minutes

Ingredients Needed:

- Garlic (2 cloves)
- Roughly chopped green onions (.5 cup)
- Tightly-packed fresh spinach (1 cup)
- Roughly chopped parsley - leaves & stems (.5 cup)
- Lemon juice (2 tsp.)
- Softened butter (.5 cup/1 stick)
- Pernod or another anise-flavored liqueur (2 tbsp.)
- Panko breadcrumbs (.75 cup)
- Freshly grated parmesan (.25 cup)
- Olive oil (1 tbsp.)
- Fresh oysters (24 - shucked & shells reserved)
- To Serve: Lemon wedges
- Coarse salt (1 lb./as needed)

Preparation Technique:

1. Adjust the oven rack to the upper-most portion and warm it at 450° Fahrenheit.
2. Mince/chop the garlic, spinach, green onions, parsley, lemon juice, butter, and pour the chosen liqueur to a food processor. Pulse the fixings until finely chopped.
3. Combine the parmesan, breadcrumbs, and oil in a mixing container.

4. Sprinkle coarse salt over a large baking sheet to a depth of ½-inch.
5. Arrange the oysters in half shells in the salt. Portion the spinach mixture among the oysters and sprinkle with the parmesan mixture.
6. Bake the oysters until the spinach mixture is bubbling, and panko is deeply golden (8 min.).
7. Serve with lemon for sprinkling if desired.

Roasted Salmon

Servings Provided: 4
Time Required: 30 minutes

Ingredients Needed:

- Wild salmon fillets (4 - 6-oz.)
- Freshly ground black pepper
- Garlic (4 cloves)
- Fresh dill (.25 cup)
- Lemon (1)

Preparation Technique:

1. Use a nonstick cooking spray to coat a glass baking dish. Warm the oven temperature at 400° Fahrenheit.
2. Slice the lemon into wedges. Add the salmon to the baking dish and squeeze the lemon over them.
3. Mince the garlic and dill to combine with the black pepper for flavoring. Sprinkle it over the fish.
4. Bake about 20-22 minutes until the center of the salmon is opaque.
5. Serve with a wedge of lemon and your favorite side dish.

Rum-Glazed Shrimp

Servings Provided: 4-6
Time Required: 45 minutes

Ingredients Needed:

- Shrimp (1.5 lb.)
- Olive oil - divided (3 tbsp.)
- Soy sauce (.25 cup)
- Sweet chili sauce (.33 cup)
- Captain Morgan Spiced Rum (.25 cup)
- Garlic (2 minced cloves)
- Juice of 1 lime
- Crushed red pepper flakes (.5 tsp.)
- To Garnish: Green onion (1 thinly sliced)

Preparation Technique:

1. Peel and devein the shrimp into a mixing container.
2. In another container, mix two tablespoons of oil with the sweet chili sauce, rum, lime juice, garlic, red pepper flakes, and soy sauce.
3. Pour ¾ of the marinade into the shrimp bowl; marinate in the fridge for 15 minutes to half of an hour.
4. Warm the oil (1 tbsp.) in a large pan using the med-high heat setting. Toss in the shrimp and cook on one side until golden (2 min.).
5. Using tongs, flip the shrimp and brush with the rest of the marinade. Cook it for another minute or two.

6. Garnish with green onions and serve promptly for the best results.

Chapter 6: Pork Favorites

Creamy Paprika Pork

Servings Provided: 4
Time Required: 30 minutes

Ingredients Needed:

- Pork tenderloin (1 lb.)
- Salt (.75 tsp.)
- A-P flour (1 tsp.)
- Paprika (4 tsp.)
- Black pepper (.25 tsp.)
- Butter (1 tbsp.)
- Heavy whipping cream (.75 cup)
- Hot rice or egg noodles

Preparation Technique:

1. Slice the pork into one-inch cubes and toss it with the flour and seasonings.
2. In a large skillet, warm the butter using the medium temperature setting. Sauté the pork until lightly browned (four to five min.).
3. Pour in the cream. Once it's boiling, stir the mixture to loosen the browned bits from the pan. Cook it without a lid until the cream is slightly thickened (five to seven min.).
4. Serve the delicious pork with noodles and a sprinkle of parsley.

Grilled Pork Chops With Smokin' Sauce

Servings Provided: 4
Time Required: 25 minutes

Ingredients Needed:

Step 1:
- Water (.25 cup)
- Ketchup (.25 cup)
- Dijon mustard (1 tbsp.)
- Worcestershire sauce (1 tsp.)
- Molasses (1 tbsp.)
- Packed brown sugar (1.5 tsp)
- Kosher salt (.25 tsp.)
- Chipotle hot pepper sauce (.25 tsp.)
- Black pepper (1/8 tsp.)

The Chops:
- Mustard seeds (1.25 tsp.)
- Whole peppercorns (1.25 tsp.)
- Garlic powder (1 tsp.)
- Cayenne pepper (.25 tsp.)
- Kosher salt (.5 tsp.)
- Smoked paprika (1.25 tsp.)
- Onion powder (1 tsp.)
- Brown sugar (1.5 tsp.)
- Bone-in pork chops (4 @ 7 oz. each)

Preparation Technique:

1. Warm a small saucepan using the medium temperature setting.

2. Whisk the 'step one' fixings. Once boiling, lower the heat and simmer, uncovered, until slightly thickened (10 min.), stirring occasionally. Reserve ¼ cup of the sauce for serving.
3. Using a spice grinder, crush the seasonings with brown sugar and rub the mixture over the chops.
4. Arrange the chops on an oiled grill (medium heat).
5. Grill, covered, until a thermometer reads 145° Fahrenheit for five to six minutes on each side, brushing the top with the remainder of the sauce after turning. Wait for about five minutes before serving with the reserved sauce.

Mango-Glazed Ham On The Grill

Servings Provided: 8
Time Required: 55 minutes

Ingredients Needed:

- Red wine vinegar (1.5 cups)
- Sugar (.5 cup)
- Jalapeno pepper (1 tsp.)
- Fresh ginger (1 tsp.)
- Mango (1 medium) or ripe peaches (2 medium)
- Fully cooked ham steak (bone out - 2 lb.)
- Pepper (1/8 tsp.)

Preparation Technique:

1. Grease the grill rack using an oily paper towel.
2. Finely mince the ginger and jalapeno. Slice and peel the peaches or mango.
3. Mix the vinegar, sugar, jalapeno, and ginger in a saucepan. Once boiling, adjust the setting to simmer - *lid on* - 25-30 minutes or until the glaze is thick and caramelized. Strain the mixture and cool.
4. Toss the mango into a food processor and pulse the fixings until they are creamy smooth. Stir the mixture into the glaze and set aside.
5. Sprinkle both sides of the ham steak with pepper.
6. Grill the ham - covered - using the medium temperature setting for about ten minutes on each side.

7. Brush the ham on all sides using the mango glaze, and grill it for another five minutes.
8. Serve the ham with the remaining glaze.

No-Fuss Pork Chops

Servings Provided: 4
Time Required: 30 minutes

Ingredients Needed:

- Pineapple juice (.5 cup)
- Cider vinegar (2 tbsp.)
- Salt (.5 tsp.)
- Brown sugar (2 tbsp.)
- Olive oil - divided (2 tbsp.)
- Boneless pork loin chops (4 @ 5 oz. each)
- Onions (2 medium)

Preparation Technique:

1. Whisk the brown sugar with the pineapple juice, vinegar, and salt.
2. Warm a skillet using the medium temperature setting. Pour in the oil and brown the chops and set aside on a platter for now.
3. In the same pan, add the remainder of the oil. Chop and toss in the onions to sauté until tender. Stir in the juice mixture and boil. Adjust the temperature to simmer, covered, for ten minutes.
4. Arrange the chops in the pan and cook, covered, until they reach an internal temperature of 145° Fahrenheit (2-3 min.).
5. Leave the chops covered for five minutes before serving with a portion of noodles (if desired) and top with green onions.

Peachy Pork Ribs

Servings Provided: 4
Time Required: 2.5 hours

Ingredients Needed:

- Baby back ribs (2 racks/4 lb.)
- Water (.5 cup)
- Ripe peaches (3 medium)
- Onion (2 tbsp.)
- Butter (2 tbsp.)
- Garlic clove (1)
- Lemon juice (3 tbsp.)
- Soy sauce (2 tsp.)
- Brown sugar (1 tbsp.)
- Orange juice concentrate (2 tbsp.)
- Ground mustard (.5 tsp.)
- Salt (.25 tsp.)

Preparation Technique:

1. Slice the ribs into serving-sized pieces and arrange in a shallow roasting pan with the water. Place a layer of foil or a lid over the pan. Bake the ribs at 325° Fahrenheit for two hours.
2. Prepare the sauce by peeling, cubing, and adding the peaches into a blender. Cover with the lid and mix until blended.
3. Chop/mince the onion and garlic.
4. Warm a saucepan to melt the butter. Sauté them a few minutes until they're tender. Stir in the orange juice concentrate, lemon juice,

brown sugar, mustard, soy sauce, pepper, salt, and peach puree. Stir until heated.
5. Drain the ribs and cover with the sauce.
6. Grill the ribs on a lightly oiled rack, covered, using the medium temperature setting for eight to ten minutes - flipping them occasionally and brushing with the tasty sauce. Serve and enjoy with your favorite veggies.

Pork Loin Steaks

Servings Provided: 2
Time Required: 25 minutes

Ingredients Needed:

- Pork loin steaks (4 boneless)
- Water (.25 cup)
- Brown sugar (2 tbsp.)
- Dried oregano (1 tsp.)

Preparation Technique:

1. Use a non-metallic container to combine the marinade fixings.
2. Add the steaks to the bowl and cover to marinate overnight or for a minimum of two hours in the fridge.
3. Prepare the grill using the med-high temperature setting.
4. Grill the steaks for three to five minutes on each side and serve with your favorite side dishes.

Pork Medallions With Garlic-Strawberry Sauce

Servings Provided: 4
Time Required: 25 minutes

Ingredients Needed:

- Fresh strawberries (2 cups - whole)
- Water (.25 cup)
- Chicken bouillon granules (1 tsp.)
- A-P flour (.5 cup)
- Eggs (2 large)
- Seasoned breadcrumbs (2/3 cup)
- Pork tenderloin (1 lb.)
- Salt (.25 tsp.)
- Black pepper (.25 tsp.)
- Butter - divided (6 tbsp.)
- Garlic (1 tsp.)
- Optional: Freshly sliced strawberries

Preparation Technique:

1. Pour water, whole strawberries, and bouillon in a food processor, pulsing until blended.
2. Prepare three shallow bowls: One each; for flour, eggs, and the third with breadcrumbs.
3. Slice the pork into ½-inch slices, and pound each with a meat mallet to reach a ¼-inch thickness. Sprinkle it with pepper and salt.
4. Dip the pork in flour to coat both sides and shake off any excess.
5. Dip it into eggs; lastly, in the crumbs.

6. Warm a large skillet using the med-high temperature setting to melt two tablespoons of the butter. Add the pork and cook until tender (2-3 min. each side). Dump it into a bowl and keep warm.
7. Mince and sauté the garlic in the rest of the butter for one minute (same pan). Stir in the strawberry mixture and thoroughly heat it.
8. Serve the pork with the tasty sauce. Garnish it using a few strawberries.

Southern-Style Pork Tenderloin Fajitas

Servings Provided: 4
Time Required: 25 minutes

Ingredients Needed:

- Pork tenderloin (1 lb.)
- Chili powder (.5 tsp.)
- Fresh cilantro (.25 cup)
- Ground cumin (.5 tsp.)
- Garlic powder (.5 tsp.)
- Canola oil (1 tbsp.)
- Onion (1 small)
- Green pepper - julienned (1 medium)
- Warmed flour tortillas (4 @ 8-inches)
- Optional: Sour cream & shredded cheddar cheese

Preparation Technique:

1. Thinly slice the pork. Mince the cilantro and slice the onions into rings.
2. Whisk the cilantro, garlic powder, chili powder, and cumin.
3. Prepare a large frying pan with oil to sauté the pork until done. Stir in the rings of onion and sliced pepper, cooking until crispy and tender.
4. Toss them with the seasoning mixture.
5. Spoon the mixture over the tortillas to serve with cheese and sour cream as desired.

Chapter 7: Pasta Favorites

Classic Baked Macaroni & Cheese

Servings Provided: 6-8
Time Required: 47-50 minutes

Ingredients Needed:

- Milk (2 cups)
- Butter (2 tbsp.)
- A-P flour (2 tbsp.)
- Salt (.5 tsp.)
- Black pepper (.25 tsp.)
- Extra-sharp shredded cheddar cheese (10 oz. block)
- Optional: Ground red pepper (.25 tsp.)
- Cooked elbow macaroni (8 oz. pkg.)
- Also Needed: Lightly greased 2-quart baking dish

Preparation Technique:

1. Prepare the pasta and set it aside to keep warm.
2. Warm the oven at 400° Fahrenheit.
3. Melt butter in a dutch oven using the med-low heat. Whisk in the flour until it's smooth and simmer for about two minutes. Gradually whisk in milk, cooking about five minutes until thickened. Remove the pan from the hot

burner and mix in salt, black pepper, one cup shredded cheese, red pepper, and cooked pasta.
4. Spoon the pasta mixture into the baking dish and top with the rest of the cheese (one cup).
5. Bake it until bubbly (20 min.). Allow the pasta and cheese to stand for about ten minutes before serving.

Elbow Macaroni & Vegetable Toss

Servings Provided: 4-6
Time Required: 30 minutes

Ingredients Needed:

- Elbow macaroni - whole-wheat (8 oz.)
- Frozen peas (1 cup)
- Zucchini (3 cups)
- Small broccoli florets (3 cups)
- Red pepper (1)
- Onion (1 cup)
- Prepared basil pesto (.33 cup)
- Grated parmesan cheese (.66 cup)

Preparation Technique:

1. Prepare a pot of water and cook the macaroni per the package instructions, adding peas in the last minute of cooking. Drain, reserving 2/3 cup of the cooking liquid.
2. Warm a large skillet to cook the pesto using one-third cup of the cooking liquid. Chop and mix in the broccoli, zucchini, red pepper, and onion. Cook them with the lid on until the veggies are fork-tender (3 min.).
3. Fold in the macaroni and rest of the cooking liquid to the skillet. Mix until the macaroni and vegetables are coated using the parmesan cheese.

Mason Jar Pasta Salad

Servings Provided: 4
Time Required: 20 minutes

Ingredients Needed:

- Farfalle (4 oz.)
- Low-fat baby bocconcini cheese (4 oz.)
- Halved heirloom cherry tomatoes (5 oz.)
- Cucumber (1 cup)
- Red pepper (1 cup)
- Red onion (.5 cup)
- Baby spinach (2 cups)

The Vinaigrette:

- Olive oil (3 tbsp.)
- Salt & pepper (.25 tsp. each)
- Dijon mustard (1 tsp.)
- Dried oregano (.5 tsp.)
- Red wine vinegar (4 tsp.)
- Fresh parsley (1 tbsp.)

Preparation Technique:

1. Chop the parsley, cucumber, red pepper, and onion. Prepare the pasta per the package instructions. Dump it into a colander to drain and cool.
2. Portion the pasta and cheese into four eight-ounce Mason jars.
3. Toss the tomatoes, cucumber, red pepper, and onion. Divide those among jars.

4. Whisk the oil, parsley, vinegar, mustard, salt, pepper, and oregano.
5. Sprinkle the vinaigrette over the tomato mixture, topping it off with spinach. Cover and refrigerate the delicious mixture for up to four hours. Toss gently before serving.

New Orleans Sausage Shrimp Crawfish Pasta

Servings Provided: 4
Time Required: 35 minutes

Ingredients Needed:

- Raw shrimp (12 oz./small-sized)
- Andouille smoked sausage (14 oz.)
- Crawfish (12 oz.)
- Butter (.5 cup)
- Onion (.5 cup)
- Garlic (2 cloves)
- All-purpose flour (.25 cup)
- Tomato sauce (4 tbsp.)
- Water (1 cup)
- Hot sauce (3 dashes)
- Cajun seasoning (1.5 tsp. + 1 tbsp. or to taste)
- Green onions (6)
- Pepper & salt (as desired)
- Elbow macaroni (8 oz.)

Preparation Technique:

1. Chop the garlic and onion.
2. Drain the crawfish.
3. Slice and cook the sausage for seven to eight minutes. Place it on a platter when done.
4. Rinse and peel the shrimp. Place them into a pan to simmer for three to four minutes until thoroughly cooked. Toss in the crawfish and

simmer for three to four minutes and remove from the pan.
5. Adjust the temperature setting to medium and melt the butter to melt. Sauté the onion for about five minutes or until it's translucent, adding the garlic to simmer for one more minute.
6. Whisk in the flour until combined. Mix in the water and tomato sauce. Simmer until the sauce starts thickening (5 min.).
7. Fold in the sausage, shrimp, and crawfish to simmer for about five minutes.
8. Mince and add the green onions, salt, hot sauce, pepper, and cajun seasoning.
9. Serve the sauce over your favorite pasta noodles.

Shrimp Monica - Original Crawfish & Noodles

Servings Provided: 4
Time Required: 40 minutes

Ingredients Needed:

- Pasta - Penne, bowties, rotini, linguine, fettuccine (1 lb.)
- Crawfish tails & fat - Louisiana-style/not Chinese (1 lb.)
- Butter - not margarine (1 stick)
- Half & Half (1 pint)
- Green onion (1 large bunch & tops)
- Minced garlic (1-2 tbsp.)
- Salt & Creole seasoning (as desired)

Preparation Technique:

1. Prepare a pot of salted water to cook the pasta until its al dente. Rinse it in cool water and drain in a colander.
2. Prepare a skillet to melt the butter. Mince and sauté the onions and garlic for three minutes.
3. Fold in the raw shrimp with the garlic and onions. Mix in the crawfish and Half & Half and simmer until it's bubbly.
4. Mix in the creole seasoning and salt, adjusting as desired by taste.
5. Add the crawfish and simmer using the medium temperature setting for five to ten minutes.

6. Toss in the pasta and simmer (low heat) for about ten minutes. Stir often and serve promptly with French bread and a delicious glass of white wine!

Are you enjoying this book? If so, I'd be really happy if you could leave a short review, it means a lot to me! Thank you.

Chapter 8: Salad Favorites

California Avocado Salad

Servings Provided: 8
Time Required: 20 minutes

Ingredients Needed:

- Medium oranges (3)
- Toasted pine nuts (.25 cup)
- Medium ripe avocados (2)
- Rosemary (1 pinch)

Preparation Technique:

1. Peel and section the oranges and avocados and place them on a platter.
2. Scatter the mixture using the pine nuts and rosemary.
3. Enjoy the delicious salad with your favorite dressing to serve.

California Quinoa Salad

Servings Provided: 4
Time Required: 30 minutes

Ingredients Needed:

- Olive oil (1 tbsp.)
- Quinoa (1 cup)
- Garlic (2 cloves)
- Zucchini (1 medium)
- Water (2 cups)
- Canned chickpeas/garbanzo beans (.75 cup)
- Tomato (1 medium)
- Crumbled feta cheese (.5 cup)
- Greek olives (.25 cup)
- Fresh basil (2 tbsp.)
- Black pepper (.25 tsp.)

Preparation Technique:

1. Rinse and thoroughly drain the quinoa and beans.
2. Mince the garlic and basil. Chop the zucchini, olives, and tomato.
3. Prepare a saucepan to heat the oil using the med-high temperature setting.
4. Mix in the quinoa and garlic. Simmer and stir it for two to three minutes or until the quinoa is lightly browned. Stir in the zucchini and water.
5. Wait for the mixture to boil. Lower the temperature setting to simmer with the *lid on* until the liquid is absorbed (12-15 min.).

6. Add the remainder of the fixings and thoroughly warm before serving.

Classic Chicken Salad

Servings Provided: 4
Time Required: 30 minutes

Ingredients Needed:

- Mayonnaise (.5 cup)
- Dill pickle (1 small - chopped - 0.5 cup) + Pickle brine (2 tbsp.)
- Kosher salt & black pepper (as desired)
- Fresh flat-leaf parsley (2 tbsp.)
- Celery (2 stalks)
- Fresh dill (2 tbsp.)
- Boneless - skinless chicken breast (1.5 lb.)

Preparation Technique:

1. Chop the celery, pickle, dill, and parsley. Set aside.
2. Prepare a medium-sized saucepan half full of water. Once boiling, add one teaspoon of salt and the chicken. Lower the temperature setting and simmer until done (12-15 min.). Cool and shred/chop into smaller pieces.
3. Prepare the salad. Whisk the mayo and pickle brine, salt, pepper, celery, pickles, dill, parsley in a bowl. Mix in the chicken and serve.

Classic Cobb Salad

Servings Provided: 4
Time Required: 20 minutes

Ingredients Needed:

- Iceberg lettuce (6 cups)
- Tomatoes (2 medium)
- Medium ripened avocado (1)
- Cooked ham (.75 cup)
- Hard-boiled eggs (2 large)
- Cooked turkey (.75 cup)
- Fresh mushrooms (1.25 cups)
- Crumbled blue cheese (.5 cup)
- Salad dressing (your preference)

Optional Ingredients:

- Ripe olives
- Lemon wedges

Preparation Technique:

1. Tear the lettuce and arrange it on a platter. Boil the eggs and let them cool
2. Peel and chop the avocado. Slice the mushrooms, olives, and lemon wedges. Chop/dice the tomatoes, ham, turkey, and eggs.

Crab Louie Lettuce Wraps

Servings Provided: 12
Time Required: 30 minutes

Ingredients Needed:

- Sour cream (1 cup)
- Sweet chili sauce (.5 cup)
- Lime juice (1 tbsp.)
- Ground cumin (.25 tsp.)
- Fresh ginger root (2 tbsp.)
- Lump crabmeat (6 oz. can)
- Boston/Bibb lettuce (12 leaves)
- Medium mangoes (2)
- Green onions (4)
- Medium carrot (1)
- Fresh cilantro leaves (.25 cup)
- Toasted sesame seeds (2 tbsp.)
- Fresh mint leaves (.25 cup)

Preparation Technique:

1. Mince the ginger. Peel and thinly slice the onions, mangos, and avocados.
2. Shred the carrot and chop the mint.
3. Drain and squeeze dry the crabmeat.
4. Combine the sour cream, chili sauce, ginger, ground cumin, and lime juice.
5. Serve it by placing one tablespoon of the crab onto each leaf of lettuce. Top it off using the rest of the fixings.

6. Spritz it using the delicious dressing and serve with the rest of the sauce on the side.

Grilled Southwestern Pasta & Steak Salad

Servings Provided: 4
Time Required: 45 minutes

Ingredients Needed:

- Beef top sirloin steak (.75 lb.)
- Ground cumin (.25 tsp.)
- Black pepper & salt (.25 tsp. of each)
- Poblano peppers (3)
- Fresh sweet corn - in husks (2 large ears)
- Sweet onion (1 large)
- Olive oil (1 tbsp.)
- Multigrain bow tie pasta (2 uncooked cups)
- Tomatoes (2 large)
  The Dressing:
- Olive oil (1 tbsp.)
- Lime juice (.25 cup)
- Salt (.25 tsp.)
- Ground cumin (.25 tsp.)
- Fresh cilantro (.33 cup)
- Black pepper (.25 tsp.)

Preparation Technique:

1. Combine the salt, cumin, and pepper; rub the steak.
2. Remove the husks from the corn and slice the onions into ½-inch rings. Slice the peppers and discard the seeds. Brush poblano peppers, corn, and onion with oil.

3. Use a meat mallet to pound the steak until it's about one inch thick.
4. Grill the steak, covered, using the medium temperature setting on the grill or broil it in the oven about four inches from the burner for six to eight minutes per side. For medium-rare, an internal thermometer should read 135° Fahrenheit; medium, 140° Fahrenheit or; medium-well, 145° Fahrenheit).
5. Prepare the pasta until it's al dente. Grill the veggies (also covered) for eight to ten minutes, turning occasionally.
6. Remove the corn from the cob, and coarsely chop the peppers, onions, and tomatoes. Transfer the vegetables into a large salad container.
7. Prepare the dressing by whisking the lime juice, oil, salt, cumin, and pepper until blended. Lastly, stir in cilantro.
8. Drain the pasta and toss it with the veggie mixture. Drizzle with dressing, tossing to coat. Slice the prepared steak into thin slices, and add to the salad.

Southern Cornbread Salad

Servings Provided: 16
Time Required: 30 minutes + chill time

Ingredients Needed:

- Cornbread/muffin mix (8.5 oz. pkg.)
- Mayonnaise (1 cup)
- Ranch salad dressing mix (1 envelope)
- Sour cream (1 cup)
- Tomatoes (3 large)
- Sweet bell peppers - 1 each red & green (.5 cup each)
- Green onions (1 cup - thinly sliced)
- Pinto beans (2 - 15 oz. cans)
- Shredded cheddar cheese (2 cups)
- Cooked-crumbled bacon (10 strips)
- Frozen - thawed corn (3.5 cups)
- Also Needed: 3-quart glass bowl

Preparation Technique:

1. Chop the tomatoes, peppers, and onions Rinse and drain the beans.
2. Prepare the cornbread mix according to package directions. Bake it using an eight-inch square baking dish. When it's cool, break it apart until crumbly
3. Mix the sour cream, salad dressing, and mayo until blended.
4. Toss the peppers, tomatoes, and ½ cup of green onions into another container.

5. Prepare the glass salad dish by layering half of each; the cornbread, tomato mix, cheese, beans, corn, bacon, and dressing.
6. Repeat the layers. Top with remaining green onions. Refrigerate for about three hours.

Southwestern Pork Salad

Servings Provided: 4
Time Required: 15 minutes + chill time

Ingredients Needed:

- Pork loin strips (2 cups)
- Kidney beans (16 oz. can)
- Onion (1 medium)
- Tomato (1 large)
- Green pepper (1 large)
- Ripe olives (.5 cup)
- Cider vinegar (.25 cup)
- Canola oil (.25 cup)
- Sugar (2 tbsp.)
- Ground mustard (1 tsp.)
- Ground cumin (1 tsp.)
- Fresh parsley (2 tbsp)
- Salt (.5 tsp.)
- Oregano - dried (1 tsp.)

Preparation Technique:

1. Rinse and drain the beans and slice the olives. Chop the tomato, peppers, and onions. Mince the parsley.
2. Toss the pork, onion peppers, onions, olives, and tomatoes into a large salad container. Whisk the rest of the fixings to dress the salad and pop it into the fridge to chill for four to six hours. Stir occasionally to mix the flavors.

Waldorf Salad

Servings Provided: 6
Time Required: 10 minutes

Ingredients Needed:

- Honeycrisp/Gala apples (2 large/3 cups)
- Celery (2 cups)
- Raisins (.25 cup)
- Toasted walnuts (.25 cup)
- Plain yogurt (.33 cup)
- Reduced-fat mayo (.33 cup)

Preparation Technique:

1. Chop the apples (peel on), celery, and toasted walnuts.
2. Toss them with the raisins.
3. Mix in the yogurt and mayo, tossing to mix.
4. Place the bowl in the fridge - covered - until time to serve.

Chapter 9: Soup Favorites

Best Ever Beef Stew - Slow-Cooked

Servings Provided: 8 - varies
Time Required: 8 hours 20 minutes

Ingredients Needed:

- Beef stew meat (2 lb.)
- A-P flour (.5 cup)
- Black pepper (.5 tsp.)
- Seasoning salt (1 tbsp.)
- Olive oil (2 tbsp.)
- Onion (1 large)
- Bay leaves (2)
- Worcestershire sauce (.25 cup)
- Water (2 cups)
- Beef Swanson® Flavor Boost (2 heaping tsp.)
- Red-skinned potatoes (4 medium to large - peeled)
- Carrots (3 large - peeled)
- Celery (1 stalk)

Preparation Technique:

1. Prepare a resealable plastic bag with the seasoning salt, pepper, and flour. Toss to coat the beef.
2. Warm the oil in a frying pan to brown the meat and add it to the slow cooker.

3. Dice and sauté the onion in the same pan for about two minutes, tossing them into the slow cooker.
4. Pour the water, Worcestershire sauce, & beef 'flavor boost' into the skillet.
5. Whisk - as you scrape up any browned bits from the pan. Remove it to the countertop for now.
6. Dice and add the carrots, celery, potatoes, bay leaves, and the broth mixture into the crockpot.
7. Securely close the top and simmer using the low setting for eight hours. Remove the bay leaves before serving.

Brunswick Stew

Servings Provided: 6
Time Required: 60 minutes

Ingredients Needed:

- Olive oil (1 tbsp.)
- Onion (1)
- Garlic (2 cloves)
- Carrots (2)
- Celery (.75 cup)
- Red-skinned potatoes (2 small)
- Corn (2 cups - frozen)
- Lima beans (1 cup - frozen)
- Diced tomatoes (28 oz. can)
- Low-sodium chicken broth (32 oz. carton)
- Dried parsley (1 tsp.)
- Bay leaf (1)
- Worcestershire sauce (2 tbsp.)
- Shredded chicken (2.5 cups)
- Black pepper & salt (1 tsp. each)
- Hot sauce (.5 tsp.) *To Serve:*
- Hot sauce
- Fresh parsley

Preparation Technique:

1. Rinse and drain the limas and corn.
2. Warm the oil using the medium temperature setting in a dutch oven. Mince the onion and

garlic, and toss them into the pan. Sauté them until fragrant and soft.
3. Chop and add in carrots, celery and potatoes, canned tomatoes, broth, corn, lima beans, Worcestershire sauce, parsley, bay leaf, salt, pepper, and hot sauce.
4. Once it's boiling, adjust the temperature setting to simmer for until the potatoes are tender (30-45 min.). Stir occasionally.
5. Discard the bay leaf and add in shredded chicken, stir to combine, and cook for another five minutes or until the chicken is heated thoroughly.
6. Once the stew is ready to serve, scoop it into serving bowls and garnish as desired.
7. Special Tip: If the stew seems too thin, mash some of the potatoes with a fork to create a thicker broth. If the stew is too thick, mix in a bit more water or chicken broth, starting with about ½ of a cup.

Cabbage Roll Soup

Servings Provided: 8
Time Required: 60 minutes

Ingredients Needed:

- Olive oil (1 tbsp.
- Lean ground beef (1.5 lb.)
- Freshly cracked pepper & salt
- Yellow onion (1 large/1.75 cups)
- Carrots (2 large/1.25 cup)
- Packed cabbage (5 cups/16-19 oz.)
- Garlic (3 cloves)
- Beef broth - low-sodium (2 cans @ 14.5 oz. each)
- Tomato sauce (3 cans @ 8 oz. each)
- Petite diced tomatoes (2 cans @ 14.5 oz. each)
- Worcestershire sauce (1 tbsp.)
- Oregano (dried - 1 tsp.) or (fresh - 1 tbsp.)
- Brown sugar (2 tbsp. - packed)
- Dried paprika (1.5 tsp.)
- Bay leaves (2)
- Thyme (dried - .75 tsp.) or (fresh - 2.5 tsp.)
- Fresh lemon juice (1 tbsp.)
- Long-grain white rice (.75 cup - dry)
- Fresh parsley (1/3 cup)

Preparation Technique:

1. Chop the onions, garlic, carrots, cabbage, thyme, oregano, and parsley. Set aside to use.

2. Prepare a cast-iron skillet using the med-high temperature setting to warm one tablespoon of oil.
3. Once the skillet is sizzling hot, add the beef, pepper, and salt. Break it apart while browning and dump it onto a towel-lined plate, reserving two tablespoons of the fat.
4. Toss the carrots and onion into the pan and sauté for one minute. Fold in the cabbage and sauté another two minutes. Add the garlic to sauté one more minute.
5. Dump the bay leaves, thyme oregano, paprika, Worcestershire, brown sugar, tomato sauce, beef broth, salt, pepper, and tomatoes. Also, add the beef back into the soup.
6. Once boiling, mix in the rice and cover the pot, and adjust the temperature setting to simmer for 25 minutes.
7. Stir in more broth and one cup of water to thin as desired.
8. Serve with a spritz of lemon juice and parsley.

Cheeseburger Soup

Servings Provided: 8/2 quarts
Time Required: 55 minutes

Ingredients Needed:

- Ground beef (.5 lb.)
- Butter - divided (4 tbsp.)
- Basil (1 tsp. - dried)
- Onion (.75 cup)
- Carrots (.75 cup)
- Parsley flakes (1 tsp. - dried)
- Potatoes (4 cups/1.75 lb.)
- Chicken broth (3 cups)
- A-P flour (.25 cup)
- Shredded Velveeta (2-4 cups/as desired)
- Whole milk (1.5 cups)
- Salt (.75 tsp.)
- Black pepper (.25-.5 tsp.)
- Sour cream (.25 cup)

Preparation Technique:

1. Chop the onion, celery, and carrots. Peel and cube the potatoes.
2. Prepare a large saucepan using the medium temperature setting. Toss in the beef and simmer until it's thoroughly done, drain the fats, and set aside.
3. Melt one tablespoon of butter in the pan to sauté the carrots, celery, onions, parsley, and basil until the veggies are tender (10 min.).

4. Mix in the potatoes, beef, and broth. Once boiling, adjust the temperature setting and simmer, covered until the potatoes are tender (9-13 min.).
5. Prepare a skillet and melt the rest of the butter. Mix in the flour, cook, and stir until bubbly (3-5 min.).
6. Simmer the mixture for two minutes and adjust the temperature setting to low. Mix in the milk, cheese, pepper, and salt.
7. After the cheese is melted, transfer the soup from the hot burner and mix in the sour cream to serve.

Cheesy Ham Chowder

Servings Provided: 10
Time Required: 1 hour

Ingredients Needed:

- Bacon (10 strips)
- Onion (1 large)
- Carrots (1 cup)
- A-P flour (3 tbsp.)
- Water (1.5 cups)
- Whole milk (3 cups)
- Potatoes (2.5 cups)
- Whole kernel corn (15.25 oz. can)
- Chicken bouillon granules (2 tsp.)
- Shredded cheddar cheese (3 cups)
- Pepper (as desired)
- Fully-cooked ham (2 cups - cubed)

Preparation Technique:

1. Drain the corn in a colander and set it aside.
2. Cook the bacon using the medium temperature setting in a Dutch oven. Transfer it to a layer of paper towels and set it aside to drain.
3. Dice the carrots and onions. Toss them into the pan drippings to sauté until tender. Whisk in the flour, and slowly mix in the water and milk.
4. Wait for it to boil and cook it until thickened (2 min.).
5. Peel, chop, and add the potatoes, bouillon, pepper, and drained corn.

6. Lower the temperature setting and simmer with the lid off until the potatoes are tender (20 min.).
7. Add in the ham and cheese. Chop and stir in the bacon to serve.

Creamy Chicken Noodle Soup - Slow-Cooked

Servings Provided: 8
Time Required: High/3-4 hours & 20 minutes or Low: 6-8 hours

Ingredients Needed:

- Water (3 cups)
- Chicken broth - low-sodium preferred (32 oz.)
- Cooked chicken (2.5 cups)
- Dried thyme (1.5 tsp.) crushed
- Carrots (1.5 cups)
- Onion (.25 cup)
- Sliced mushrooms (1.5 cups)
- Celery (1.5 cups)
- Garlic pepper (.75 tsp.)
- Cream cheese - Neufchatel - diced & low-fat (3 oz.)
- Egg noodles - dry (2 cups)
- Suggested Cooker Size: 5-6 quarts

Preparation Technique:

1. Chop the veggies and cooked chicken into cubes and add them to the cooker with the water, celery, carrots, mushrooms, onion, thyme, and garlic pepper.
2. Securely close the lid and select the chosen times.
3. Note: If you choose the low-temperature setting, turn the cooker to the high setting.

4. Mix in the cream cheese, folding in the uncooked noodles. Place the lid on the pot and simmer for 20 minutes to half an hour or until the noodles are cooked as you like them.

Potato Beer Cheese Soup

Servings Provided: 2 quarts/8 servings
Time Required: 55 minutes

Ingredients Needed:

- Potatoes (6 medium/2 lb.)
- Onion (1 small)
- Water (2 cups)
- 2% milk (1.5 cups)
- Chicken broth/beer (1 cup)
- Worcestershire sauce (2 tbsp.)
- Chicken bouillon cubes (2)
- Salt (.75 tsp.)
- Ground mustard (.5 tsp.)
- White pepper (.5 tsp.)
- Shredded cheddar cheese (2 cups)

Preparation Technique:

1. Peel and dice the onion and potatoes. Dump them into a pot of water. Wait for it to boil and adjust the temperature setting, covering to cook for 15-20 minutes until tender.
2. Transfer it from the burner and slightly cool - don't drain. Dump it into a blender, cover, and process mixture in batches until smooth. Transfer all of the soup back into the pan and thoroughly warm it.
3. Mix in the milk, Worcestershire sauce, beer, salt, bouillon, white pepper, and mustard.

4. Fold in the cheese just until melted. Garnish it to your liking using croutons, bacon, chives, and pepper.

Sausage & Chicken Gumbo - Slow-Cooked

Servings Provided: 6
Time Required: 6 hours 35 minutes

Ingredients Needed:

- A-P flour (.25 cup)
- Canola oil (.25 cup)
- Chicken broth - divided (4 cups)
- Smoked sausage (14 oz. pkg.)
- Frozen-thawed okra (1 cup)
- Green pepper (1 small)
- Celery (1 rib)
- Onion (1 medium)
- Garlic (3 cloves)
- Pepper (.5 tsp.)
- Salt (.25 tsp.)
- Cayenne pepper (.25 tsp.)
- Coarsely shredded cooked chicken (2 cups)
- Side Dish: Cooked rice
- Suggested Cooker Size: 4-5-quarts

Preparation Technique:

1. Cut the sausage into ½-inch slices and mince the cloves. Thaw and slice the okra. Chop the peppers, onions, and celery.
2. Whisk the oil with the flour in a heavy saucepan using the medium temperature setting about four minutes until lightly browned.

3. Adjust the temperature to med-low and simmer about 15 minutes until it is a darker reddish-brown.
4. Stir in the broth and pour into the slow cooker. Fold in the veggies, sausage, seasonings, and garlic.
5. Securely close the lid and set the timer for six to eight hours.
6. Mix in the cooked chicken and rest of the broth. Stir and warm to serve with a dish of rice!

Seafood Soup

Servings Provided: 4-6
Time Required: 35 minutes

Ingredients Needed:

- Oil (1 tbsp.)
- Onion (1 large)
- Garlic (6 cloves)
- Dry white wine (1 cup)
- Clam juice (1 cup)
- Diced tomatoes (28-oz. can)
- Bay leaf (1)
- Kosher salt (1 tsp.)

    Fresh Seafood (.5 lb. each):
- Shrimp
- Calamari
- Mussels
- Clams
- Optional to Garnish: Minced parsley (.25 cup)

Preparation Technique:

1. Warm the oil in a large stockpot using the med-high temperature setting.
2. Dice the onions and sauté them for three to four minutes - until tender. Mince and add the garlic to sauté for one more minute.
3. Pour in the clam juice, wine, bay leaf, salt, and tomatoes. Once boiling, adjust the temperature

setting to medium and cook for about 20 minutes.
4. Peel and devein the shrimp. Slice the calamari into rings.
5. Mix in all the seafood and stir to combine. Simmer until the shrimp is pink and thoroughly cooked (5-7 min.). The clams and mussels should also be open.
6. Garnish with parsley as desired and serve promptly

Traditional New England Clam Chowder

Servings Provided: 7
Time Required: 55 minutes

Ingredients Needed:

- Cherrystone Clams (12 fresh)
- Water (3 cups - cold)
- Bacon (2 strips)
- Onion (1 small)
- Potatoes (2 medium)
- Pepper & salt (.25 tsp. each)
- A-P flour (2 tbsp.)
- Half & Half cream (.5 cup)
- Whole milk (1 cup)

Preparation Technique:

1. Peel and finely chop the potatoes and onions.
2. Tap the clams and discard any that do not close. Put them into the water in a large saucepan. Wait for it to boil and add a top. Let it simmer for five to six minutes or until the clams open.
3. Pick the meat from clams, chopping it to bits, and set it to the side for now. Strain the liquid through a cheesecloth-lined colander to rest while you prepare the bacon.
4. Fry the bacon using the medium temperature setting until crisp and drain on a layer of paper

towels. Sauté the onion in the pan's drippings until tender.
5. Mince and add the bacon to the pan with the clam meat, salt, pepper, and reserved liquid.
6. Fold in the potatoes and lower the heat when it's boiling. Cover to simmer until potatoes are tender (10-12 min.)
7. Combine the flour and milk until smooth, slowly stirring it into the soup. Wait for it to boil. Simmer and stir for about two minutes until the soup is thickened. Gradually stir in the cream but don't boil.
8. Serve when it's hot.

Wild Rice Soup

Servings Provided: 8 or 2 quarts
Time Required: 1.5 hours

Ingredients Needed:

- Uncooked wild rice (.33 cup)
- Canola oil (1 tbsp.)
- Water (1 quart)
- Onion (1 medium)
- Celery (1 rib)
- Carrot (1 medium)
- Butter (.5 cup)
- A-P flour (.5 cup)
- Chicken broth (3 cups)
- Half & Half Cream (2 cups)
- Dried rosemary (.5 tsp.)
- Salt (1 tsp.)

Preparation Technique:

1. Chop the celery, carrots, and onions. Crush the rosemary.
2. Prepare a medium-sized saucepan and add the water, oil, and rice. Once boiling, lower the temperature setting and cover to simmer for about half an hour.
3. Melt the butter in a dutch oven. Chop/mince and toss in the carrots, celery, and onions to sauté for about two minutes.
4. Stir in the undrained rice and broth. Boil until slightly thickened for about two minutes. Lower the setting and stir in the salt, rosemary,

and cream. Simmer with the lid off until the rice is tender as desired (20 min.).

Chapter 10: Bread & Side Dish Favorites

Easy Cornbread

Servings Provided: 16
Time Required: 30 minutes

Ingredients Needed:

- Cornmeal (1 cup)
- Sugar (2 tbsp.)
- A-P flour (1 cup)
- Baking powder (1 tbsp.)
- Kosher salt (1 tsp.)
- Milk (1 cup)
- Egg (1 large)
- Vegetable oil (1/3 cup)
- Also Needed: 8 x 8-inch baking dish

Preparation Technique:

1. Warm the oven at 400° Fahrenheit. Lightly grease the baking dish.
2. Whisk the cornmeal, baking powder, flour, salt, and sugar.
3. Use another container to whisk the egg, oil, and milk.
4. Stir all of the fixings into one container to combine.
5. Dump the batter into the greased dish to bake for 20 to 25 minutes until it is golden brown.

Southern-Style Biscuits

Servings Provided: 10 biscuits
Time Required: 20-25 minutes

Ingredients Needed:

- All-purpose flour (2 cups)
- Cold butter (4 tbsp.)
- Salt (.5 tsp.)
- Baking powder (4 tsp.)
- Baking soda (.25 tsp.)
- Low-fat buttermilk (1 cup)

Preparation Technique:

1. Warm the oven at 425° Fahrenheit. Place a rack in the center-most position.
2. Whisk the baking powder, salt, flour, butter, and baking soda in a large mixing container.
3. Break the butter apart with your hands - mashing it into the flour to create crumbly pebbles.
4. Once combined, make a well in the center of the mixture and pour in the buttermilk. Work the dough and scoop it onto a floured surface and knead it into a square.
5. Roll it out to form a one-inch-thick circle.
6. Use a round cookie cutter to cut out the biscuits. Reshape the dough into another circle and repeat.
7. Arrange the biscuits on a baking tray coated with a spritz of cooking oil spray.

8. Bake them until nicely browned (10-12 min.).

Cauliflower Casserole

Servings Provided: 4
Time Required: 50 minutes

Ingredients Needed:

- Cauliflower (1 large head/3 lb.)
- Mushrooms (2 cups)
- Celery (.33 cup)
- Butter (.25 cup)
- Flour - all-purpose (2 tbsp.)
- Salt (.5 tsp.)
- Dry mustard (.5 tsp.)
- Milk (1.25 cups)
- Cheddar cheese- mild/sharp/ your choice - grated (1 cup)
- Breadcrumbs or soda cracker crumbs (.5 cup)
- Butter - melted (2 tbsp.)
- Also Needed: 1.5-quart baking dish

Preparation Technique:

1. Warm the oven at 350° Fahrenheit. Lightly-butter the baking dish.
2. Rinse the cauliflower and discard the tough outer leaves. Break it into small florets.
3. Steam the florets until just tender (4-6 min.). Dump them into a colander to drain. Transfer the cooked cauliflower to the baking dish and set aside.
4. Melt ¼ cup of butter in a skillet using the med-high temperature setting.

5. Slice and sauté the mushrooms and celery until tender (4-5 min.) Blend in the salt, flour, and mustard. Gradually stir in milk and cook until the mixture starts to boil. Stir in the cheese until melted. Transfer to a cool burner.
6. Pour the cheese sauce over the cauliflower and set aside.
7. Toss the cracker/breadcrumbs with two tablespoons melted butter and sprinkle it over the top of the casserole.
8. Bake it until the top is golden brown (25-30 min.). Remove from the oven and serve piping hot.

Curry With Cauliflower & Butternut Squash

Servings Provided: 4
Time Required: 30 minutes

Ingredients Needed:

- Canola oil (.5 tbsp.)
- Medium onion (1)
- Fresh ginger (.5 tbsp.)
- Cauliflower florets (1 head)
- Butternut squash** (2 cups)
- Garbanzo beans/chickpeas (14–16 oz. can)
- Jalapeño pepper (1 minced)
- Yellow curry powder (1 tbsp.)
- Diced tomatoes (14 oz. can)
- Light coconut milk (14 oz. can)
- Lime juice (1 lime)
- Black pepper & salt (as desired)
- Chopped cilantro

Preparation Technique:

1. Prepare a large pot or sauté pan using the medium-temperature setting to warm the oil.
2. Drain the beans into a colander.
3. Mince and add the ginger and onions to the oil to sauté for about two minutes until the onion is softened.
4. Cube and add the cauliflower, squash, jalapeño, garbanzos, and curry powder. Cook for about two minutes, until the veggies are covered.

5. Pour in the milk and potatoes; adjust the temperature setting to low. Add the lime juice, salt, and pepper.
6. Simmer until the veggies are fork-tender (15-20 min.).
7. Chop the cilantro and dust the veggies to serve.
8. **Potatoes or carrots would both be perfect substitutes for the squash if butternut is not in season.

Deviled Eggs

Servings Provided: 12
Time Required: 20 minutes

Ingredients Needed:

- Large eggs (1 dozen)
- Mayo (1/3 cup)
- Pickle relish (2 tbsp.) or Diced dill pickle (1)
- Dijon mustard (1.5 tsp.)
- Freshly cracked black pepper & salt (as desired)
- To Garnish: Paprika

Preparation Technique:

1. Hard boil the eggs and peel them when cooled. Slice them lengthwise and remove the yolks, tossing them into a mixing container.
2. Combine the mayo, mustard, salt, pepper, and relish, mixing it in with the yolks.
3. Mash the mixture until smooth using a fork and adjust as needed.
4. Add a scoop of the filling into each of the whites.
5. Garnish with a dusting of paprika and pop in the fridge to enjoy for up to three days.

Grits n Greens

Servings Provided: 4-6
Time Required: 60 minutes

Ingredients Needed:

- Corn oil - divided (2 tbsp.)
- Sweet onion (1 grated)
- Fresh corn kernels (.5 cup/1 ear)
- Milk (1 cup)
- Water (3 cups)
- Grits - coarsely ground (1 cup)
- Unsalted butter (2 tbsp.)
- Garlic (1 clove)
- Baby greens - ex. collard greens or kale - finely sliced in chiffonade (4 cups)
- As Desired: Freshly cracked black pepper & coarse salt

Preparation Technique:

1. Warm oil (1 tbsp.) in a saucepan using the medium temperature setting.
2. Chop and sauté the onions until transparent (2 min.). Stir in the corn and simmer, stirring occasionally, until tender (5 min.).
3. Adjust the temperature setting to med-high and add the milk and water. Once boiling, whisk in the grits, and lower the heat to low. Simmer and stir constantly until thickened (30 min.). Add two tablespoons of butter, salt, and pepper. Set it aside and keep warm.

4. Prepare a sauté pan using the high temperature setting to warm the rest of the oil (1 tbsp.). Mince and add the garlic and cook until fragrant, stirring constantly (45-60 sec.). Trim and remove the stems from and add them to the pan. Adjust the temperature setting to low, and cook until just wilted (2-3 min.).
5. Dump the grits over the greens and mix to combine.
6. Adjust the flavor using salt and pepper to your liking. Serve and enjoy them promptly.

Marinated Tomatoes, Onions & Cucumbers

Servings Provided: 4-6
Time Required: 10 minutes

Ingredients Needed:

- Cucumbers (3 medium)
- Onion (1 medium)
- Tomatoes (3 medium)
- Vinegar (.5 cup)
- Sugar (.25 cup)
- Water (1 cup)
- Salt (2 tsp.)
- Coarse black pepper (1 tsp.)
- Oil (.25 cup)

Preparation Technique:

1. Peel and slice the cucumbers to a ¼-inch thickness. Cut the tomatoes into wedges and slice the onions into rings.
2. Toss each of the fixings in a large salad container and thoroughly mix.
3. Refrigerate for a minimum of two hours before serving

<u>Northwoods Wild Rice Salad</u>

Servings Provided: 8
Time Required: 60 minutes

Ingredients Needed:

- Uncooked wild rice (2/3 cup)
- Sauerkraut (2 - 14 oz. cans)
- Chopped celery (.75 cup)
- Medium apple (1)
- Carrot (1 large/.75 cup - shredded)
- Red onion (.5 cup)

   The Dressing:

- Sugar (.5 cup)
- Cider vinegar (.33 cup)
- Canola oil (3 tbsp.)
- Black pepper & salt (.25 tsp. each)
- Fresh parsley (3 tbsp.)
- Fresh tarragon (1 tbsp.) or Dried (1 tsp.)
- Toasted - chopped walnuts (.75 cup)

Preparation Technique:

1. Prepare the rice according to package instructions and cool thoroughly. Rinse and drain the sauerkraut.
2. Prep the veggies. Chop the celery, peeled apple, and onion. Mince the parsley and tarragon, and shred the carrot.
3. Combine the sauerkraut, apple, celery, carrot, onion, and cooled rice.

4. Whisk the first five dressing fixings (to the line) until the sugar is dissolved, and stir in the herbs.
5. Combine with the sauerkraut mixture and refrigerate at least four hours (covered) for the flavors to blend.
6. Stir in walnuts just before serving.

Sausage & Mushroom Cornbread Dressing

Servings Provided: 9 cups
Time Required: 75 minutes + chill time

Ingredients Needed:

- Salt (.5 tsp.)
- Yellow cornmeal (1.5 cups)
- Baking powder (1 tsp.)
- A-P flour (.5 cup)
- Baking soda (.5 tsp.)
- 2% milk (1.5 cups)
- Large eggs (2)
- Honey (1 tbsp.)
- Olive oil - divided (.25 cup + 1 tbsp.)
- Cider vinegar (1

  tbsp.) *The Dressing*:

- Bulk pork sausage (.5 lb.)
- Freshly sliced mushrooms (8 oz.)
- Celery (3 ribs)
- Large onion (1)
- Whole wheat breadcrumbs (1.5 cups/3-4 slices - soft)
- Whisked eggs (3 large)
- Reduced-sodium chicken broth (32 oz. carton)
- Freshly minced rosemary (1 tbsp.)
- Black pepper (1 tsp.)
- Also Needed:
- Cast-iron skillet (10-inch)
- Baking dish (13 by 9-inch)

Preparation Technique:

1. Warm the oven at 425° Fahrenheit and heat the skillet.
2. Whisk the first five dry fixings up to the line.
3. In another mixing container, whisk the milk, eggs, ¼ cup of the oil, honey, and vinegar. Whisk into the dry ingredients.
4. Remove skillet from the oven and lightly grease with the remaining olive oil. Pour in the batter. Bake until golden brown (15 min.). Cool for about ten minutes; remove from pan to a wire rack to cool entirely.
5. Cook the sausage in the cast-iron skillet using the medium-high temperature setting, crumbling meat, until no longer pink. Remove and drain.
6. In the same skillet, slice/chop, and sauté the mushrooms, celery, and onion until the onion is tender (5 min.). Crumble cornbread into a large bowl; stir in the sausage, mushroom mixture, and rest of the fixings. Transfer to a greased baking dish. Refrigerate, covered, at least eight hours.
7. Remove from the refrigerator about half an hour before baking. Set the oven to 375° Fahrenheit. Bake it uncovered until the top is browned and the mixture is set (40-45 min.).

Spicy Cajun Potato Salad

Servings Provided: 20
Time Required: 30 minutes + chilling time

Ingredients Needed:

- Yukon Gold potatoes (5 lb.)
- Yellow onion (1 large)
- Lemon (half of 1 medium)
- Salt & coarsely cracked pepper (.5 tsp. each)
- Hard-boiled eggs (8)
- Mayo with olive oil (1.5 cups)
- Dill pickle relish (1 cup)
- Cajun seasoning (1-2 tbsp.)
- Yellow mustard (.25 cup)
- Fresh parsley (.25 cup)
- Paprika (1 pinch/to your liking)

Preparation Technique:

1. Peel the potatoes - chopping them into ¾-inch cubes. Toss them into a dutch oven with water. Boil and chop the egg.
2. Slice the onion in half, adding half of it to the pan. Once it's boiling, add the salt and lemon.
3. Lower the temperature setting to simmer uncovered until the potatoes are tender (5-6 min.).
4. Chop the second half of the onion and toss in with the cajun seasoning, mustard, relish, mayo, and eggs.
5. Drain and rinse the potatoes in cool water. Discard the lemon and onions.

6. Toss the eggs and potatoes. Store them in the fridge for one to two hours to cool.
7. Serve with a dusting of paprika and parsley when it's cold.

Turkey Pinto Bean Salad With Southern Molasses Dressing

Servings Provided: 6
Time Required: 35 minutes + chill time

Ingredients Needed:

- Sun-dried tomatoes - oil-packed (.5 cup)
- Garlic (1 clove)
- Molasses (.5 cup)
- Apple cider vinegar (3 tbsp.)
- Prepared mustard (1 tsp.)
- Salt (.5 tsp.)
- Coarsely ground pepper (.25 tsp.)
- Turkey breast (3 cups)
- Pinto beans (2 - 15 oz. cans)
- Green pepper (1 medium)
- Celery (2 ribs)
- Onion (1 cup)
- Fresh parsley (.25 cup)
- Optional: Lettuce leaves

Preparation Technique:

1. Rinse and drain the beans. Drain the tomatoes, reserving two tablespoons of the oil.
2. Peel and crush the garlic and tomatoes in a food processor, covering until chopped. Measure in the vinegar, molasses, mustard, salt, pepper, and reserved oil. Close the lid process until smooth.

3. Dice and toss the turkey, green pepper, celery, onions, parsley, and beans. Mix in dressing and toss.
4. Cover with plastic or foil and pop into the refrigerator chill for a couple of hours. Portion and serve on a bed of lettuce leaves as desired.

Yukon Gold & Sweet Potato Gratin

Servings Provided: 4/4-layer gratin
Time Required: 1 hour 10 minutes

Ingredients Needed:

- Yukon Gold & sweet potatoes (2 medium of each)
- Butter (2 tbsp.)
- Flour (2 tbsp.)
- 2% milk (2 cups)
- Pinch nutmeg
- Black pepper & salt
- Grated Gruyère/another Swiss cheese (.5 cup)
- Optional Garnish: Freshly chopped rosemary
- Also Needed: 8 by 8 baking dish or 10-inch cast-iron skillet

Preparation Technique:

1. Warm the oven at 375° Fahrenheit.
2. Peel and slice the potatoes into a ⅛-inch thickness.
3. Prepare a saucepan using the medium temperature setting to melt the butter.
4. Whisk in the flour, stirring for one minute.
5. Slowly whisk in the milk to prevent lumps from forming.
6. Simmer the mixture for about five minutes, until it begins to thicken like the consistency of heavy cream. Season with the nutmeg.

7. Layer the potatoes in an overlapping pattern in the bottom of a skillet/baking dish, alternating between the sweet and regular potatoes. Sprinkle each layer using the pepper and salt.
8. Pour over the sauce, then top with the grated cheese.
9. Use a layer of foil to cover the pan/dish to bake for 20 minutes.
10. Increase the temperature to 450° Fahrenheit.
11. Discard the piece of foil and bake until the top is browned as desired (approximately 20 min.).

Chapter 11: Veggie Favorites

Baked Sweet Onions

Servings Provided: 4
Time Required: 2 hours 5 minutes

Ingredients Needed:

- Vidalia sweet onions (4 large)
- Coarsely ground salt & pepper (as desired)
- Butter (4 tsp.)
- Optional: High-quality aged balsamic vinegar

Preparation Technique:

1. Set the oven temperature at 250° Fahrenheit.
2. Trim away a small portion (approximately ¼ of an inch off the bottom/root end of each onion.
3. Arrange whole onions into a baking tray with one inch of water.
4. Bake with the lid off for two hours until the onions are soft when you squeeze them.
5. Transfer them to a cutting board and pull back brown skins. Cut them off at the roots and arrange them on a serving platter with a teaspoon of butter, salt, and pepper.
6. Drizzle the tops with balsamic vinegar as desired.

BBQ Beans

Servings Provided: 16 sides
Time Required: 40 minutes
Ingredients Needed:

- Pork n Beans (2 cans - 28 oz. each)
- BBQ sauce - ex. KC Masterpiece Original (.5 cup)
- Ketchup (.5 cup)
- Yellow mustard (1 tsp.)
- Yellow onion (1 medium)
- Chili powder (1 tbsp.)
- Dark brown sugar (.5 cup)
- Freshly cracked black pepper (.5 tsp.)
- Optional Garnish: Crispy bacon

Preparation Technique:

1. Chop the onion and add with the rest of the fixings into a shallow pan.
2. Simmer the beans using the med-low temperature setting, stirring from bottom and sides frequently for until thick (30 min.).
3. Serve anytime - especially at a cookout!

Creamed Corn - Crockpot

Servings Provided: 10
Time Required: 2.5 hours

Ingredients Needed:

- Unsalted butter - divided (4 tbsp.)
- Olive oil (1 tbsp.)
- Small sweet onion (1 diced)
- Corn: See note **
- Milk - any kind you like (.5 cup)
- Honey (.5 tsp.)
- Kosher salt (.5 tbsp.)
- Black pepper (.25 tsp.)
- Reduced-fat cream cheese - not fat-free (4 oz.)
- 2% plain Greek yogurt - not nonfat (1 cup)

Preparation Technique:

1. Melt one tablespoon butter in a skillet using the med-high temperature setting.
2. Pour in the oil to heat. Mince and add the onion, sautéing it until softened and beginning to turn translucent (5 min.). Do not let the onion turn brown and adjust the heat as needed to avoid it. Transfer them to a slow cooker and add the corn.
3. Mix in the honey, milk, salt, and pepper. Dice the cream cheese and the remaining three tablespoons butter, scattering the pieces over the top, but *don't stir*. Place the lid on the crockpot and prepare using high heat for two to three hours, until the corn is hot and tender.

4. Uncover and stir until the butter, and cream cheese are well combined. Stir in the Greek yogurt. With an immersion blender, partially puree the creamed corn to thicken it. Stop to stir a few times to make sure you don't overdo it; you want the corn to be creamy but still have some nice texture to it.
5. Alternative: *In case you don't have the blender*, transfer a few ladlefuls of the creamed corn to a food processor or blender and puree (be careful, hot food splatters!). Stir the blended portion back in with the rest of the corn. Keep pureeing batches until your desired consistency is reached.
6. To further thicken the creamed corn, keep the crockpot uncovered and cook on the high-temperature setting for another 15 minutes.
7. The corn will continue to thicken as it cools down. Serve very warm - as if you were in the South!

Note **6 cups corn kernels/about 3 @ 15.25 oz. cans - drained/ 6-8 ears fresh/48 oz. frozen*

Garlic Mashed Potatoes

Servings Provided: 8
Time Required: 30 minutes

Ingredients Needed:

- Gold/red potatoes (2 lb.)
- Salt-free seasoning blend (1 tsp.)
- Olive oil (.25 cup)
- Garlic cloves (6)
- Black pepper (.5 tsp.)

Preparation Technique:

1. Scrub and dice the potatoes into large pieces.
2. Peel and add the garlic cloves and chunks of potato in a big pot filled with cold water. Once boiling, adjust the temperature setting and simmer until the potatoes are tender (20 min.). Drain the liquid, reserving ¾ cup for the next step.
3. Pour in the reserved liquid, pepper, pepper, seasoning blend, and olive oil into the potatoes and mash.
4. Serve with your favorite meat option.

Green Beans With Garlic & Peppers

Servings Provided: 6
Time Required: 10-12 minutes

Ingredients Needed:

- Olive oil (2 tsp.)
- Green beans (1 lb.)
- Red bell pepper (1)
- Red pepper flakes or chili paste (.5 tsp.)
- Garlic (1 clove)
- Sesame oil (1 tsp.)
- Black pepper (.25 tsp.)
- Salt (.5 tsp.)

Preparation Technique:

1. Trim the stems of the green beans and finely chop the garlic. Deseed and cut the bell pepper into thin slices.
2. Add the green beans to a large saucepan about ¾ full of boiling water and cook for one to three minutes until they are a vibrant green.
3. Drain the greens and add them to a pan of iced water to stop the cooking process. Set them aside.
4. Warm the oil using the medium temperature setting in a skillet. Toss in the pepper and sauté for about one minute. Toss in the beans and continue sautéing for about one more minute. Add the garlic, salt, pepper, chili paste, stirring for a minute. Drizzle using the sesame oil.

Grilled Mexican Corn

Servings Provided: 4
Time Required: 20-25 minutes

Ingredients Needed:

- Corn (4 husked ears)
- Salt (1 tsp.)
- Mayonnaise (2 tbsp.)
- Chili powder (.5 tbsp.)
- Juice of 1 lime
- Parmesan - finely grated

Preparation Technique:

1. Warm the grill until hot while you prepare a pot of salted boiling water.
2. Husk and clean the corn and toss them into the pot of boiling water.
3. Boil them for five to seven minutes, until the corn is slightly tender - not fully cooked. Drain the corn and place it onto the grill to lightly char the kernels.
4. Whisk the mayo and lime juice. Place the corn on a platter and brush it using a bit of the citrus-mayo.
5. Serve the delicious veggie with a dusting of parmesan and chili powder.

Honey Sage Carrots

Servings Provided: 4
Time Required: 10 minutes

Ingredients Needed:

- Sliced carrots (2 cups)
- Butter (2 tsp.)
- Honey (2 tbsp.)
- Freshly chopped sage (1 tbsp.)
- Black pepper (.25 tsp.)
- Salt (.125 tsp.)

Preparation Technique:

1. Peel, chop, and toss the carrots into boiling water and cook until they're fork-tender (5 min.). Drain and set aside.
2. Add the butter and toss them using pepper, sage, honey, and salt. Sauté for about three minutes, stirring frequently.
3. Serve when all is well mixed.

Southern Fried Squash

Servings Provided: 2-4
Time Required: 25 minutes

Ingredients Needed:

- Squash (2-3 medium)
- Eggs (2)
- Buttermilk (.5 cup)
- Water (4 tsp.)
- Salt and pepper (1 tsp. each/as desired)
- Unbleached flour (1 cup)
- Cornmeal (.5 cup)
- Oil for frying (as needed)
- Optional: Ranch dressing/your preference

Preparation Technique:

1. Slice the squash into a ¼-inch thickness.
2. Sift the cornmeal, flour, and seasoning in a mixing container.
3. In a separate container, whisk the eggs, water, and buttermilk.
4. Dredge each piece of squash into the seasoned flour mixture, then the wet, and back to the flour mixture.
5. Place the squash into the skillet and simmer until browned.
6. Serve with the dressing of choice.

Spicy Roasted Broccoli

Servings Provided: 8
Time Required: 30 minutes

Ingredients Needed:

- Broccoli (8 cups/1.25 lb.)
- Salt-free seasoning blend (.5 tsp.)
- Olive oil (4 tbsp. divided)
- Freshly ground black pepper (.25 tsp.)
- Garlic (4 cloves)

Preparation Technique:

1. Warm the oven at 450° Fahrenheit.
2. Trim away the large stems and cut the broccoli into two-inch pieces.
3. Mix the oil and broccoli in a mixing container. Sprinkle with pepper and seasonings as desired.
4. Move it to a baking tray with a rim and bake for 15 minutes.
5. Mince and combine the garlic, red pepper flakes, and about half of the oil in a separate dish.
6. After the broccoli is done, sprinkle the oil mixture over the broccoli while shaking the pan.
7. Put the pan back into the oven for another eight to ten minutes to finish roasting. Serve when they are tender.

Chapter 12: Pie Favorites

Pie Crust

Servings Provided: 1 crust
Time Required: 3 ¼ hours

Ingredients Needed:

- Super-cold butter (1 stick/.5 cup)
- A-P flour (1.5 cups + more for surface)
- Granulated sugar (1 tbsp.)
- Kosher salt (.25 tsp.)
- Apple cider vinegar (.5 tbsp.)
- Ice water (4 tbsp. + more as needed)

Preparation Technique:

1. Chop the butter into ½-inch chunks. Place the butter and flour into the freezer for about half an hour.
2. Sift or whisk the sugar, flour, and salt. You can do this in a food processor.
3. Add butter - using your hands - mixing until it's crumbly.
4. Mix in the vinegar and then the ice water, a little at a time, until the dough starts to form and is slightly crumbly.
5. Scoop the dough onto a lightly floured surface and work it into a flattened disk.

6. Place it in a container and cover using a layer of plastic. Pop it in the fridge to chill until it is cold (minimum of two hours or overnight).
7. Note: Double the recipe if you want a topping crust.

Apple Pie

Servings Provided: 6
Time Required: 45 minutes

Ingredients Needed:

The Crust:
- Almond flour (3 cups)
- Maple syrup (2 tbsp.)
- Egg (1 large)
- Kosher salt (.5 tsp.)
- Coconut oil (3 tbsp.)

The Filling:
- Apples (5-6 cups apples)
- Coconut oil (2 tbsp.)
- Ground cinnamon (1 tbsp.)
- Maple syrup (.25 cup)
- Arrowroot powder (1 tbsp.)
- Vanilla extract (1 tbsp.)

Preparation Technique:

1. Heat the oven at 350° Fahrenheit.
2. Combine each of the crust ingredients in a bowl until a soft dough forms. Split the dough in half and roll it out between two sheets of parchment paper. Place one half of the dough into a pie pan and gently press into the side.
3. Roll out the second half of the dough and slice into thin strips. Refrigerate the dough while you make the filling.

4. Warm the coconut oil in a large pot. Peel, chop, and sauté the apples for about five minutes. Mix in the maple syrup and cinnamon.
5. Transfer the pan to a cool burner and mix in the arrowroot powder and vanilla extract. Let it cool.
6. Spoon the cooled apple mixture into the crust.
7. Transfer the pie dough strips onto the pie to form a lattice crust by placing three strips horizontally across the pie, and three strips vertically across the pie.
8. Set a timer and bake the pie for 30 minutes. Serve hot or cold.

Big Boy Strawberry Pie

Servings Provided: 6-8
Time Required: 5-10 minutes + chill time

Ingredients Needed:

- Cornstarch (2 tbsp.)
- Water (1 cup)
- Sugar (1 cup)
- Strawberry gelatin (half of 1 pkg.)
- Pie shell (baked 9-inch - cooled)
- Fresh strawberries (approx. 5 cups)
- Whipped topping

Preparation Technique:

1. Whisk the sugar and cornstarch, and mix with the water in a saucepan.
2. Simmer for three to five minutes until thickened.
3. Transfer to a cool burner and add the gelatin, stirring to dissolve.
4. Stir in the berries and dump into the pie shell.
5. Chill for two to three hours and serve with the whipped topping as desired.

Blueberry-Custard Pie

Servings Provided: 8
Time Required: 60 minutes

Ingredients Needed:

- Unbaked pie crust (1 @ 9-inch)
- Sour cream (8 oz./1 cup)
- Sugar (.75 cup)
- Egg (1)
- Salt (.25 tsp.)
- Flour (2 tbsp.)
- Vanilla extract (2 tsp.)
- Fresh blueberries (2.5 cups) *Streusel Topping:*
- Flour (.33 cup)
- Brown sugar (.5 cup)
- Unchilled soft butter (.25 cup)
- Pecans (.5 cup - chopped)

Preparation Technique:

1. Warm the oven to reach 400º Fahrenheit.
2. Mix the egg, sour cream, sugar, two tablespoons flour, salt, and vanilla extract with a spoon until smooth. Fold the berries into the sour cream and scoop the filling into the unbaked pie crust.
3. Bake it for 25 minutes.

4. Prepare the streusel topping by combining the flour and brown sugar. Mix the butter in until it is crumbly. Fold in the chopped pecans.
5. Sprinkle the streusel crunch topping over the top of the pie when it has finished baking.
6. Bake it for another 15 to 20 minutes or until the topping is browned.
7. Transfer the pie from the oven and wait for at least 10 to 15 minutes before serving
8. Serve the pie warm or chilled.

Chess Pie

Servings Provided: 8
Time Required: 6 hours 10 minutes (includes chill time)

Ingredients Needed:

- Pie crust (1 - above recipe)
- Eggs (4 large)
- Granulated sugar (1.5 cups)
- Butter - melted and cooled slightly (.5 cup/1 stick)
- Milk (.25 cup)
- White vinegar (1 tbsp.)
- Pure vanilla extract (2 tsp.)
- Cornmeal (.25 cup)
- All-purpose flour (1 tbsp.)
- Kosher salt (.5 tsp.)
- Also Needed: 9-inch round pie dish

Preparation Technique:

1. Warm the oven at 425° Fahrenheit.
2. Roll out the pie crust and arrange it into the pie dish. Trim and crimp edges, and poke the center of the crust using a fork. Pop it into the freezer to chill for at least 15 minutes.
3. Arrange a layer of parchment baking paper inside the pie crust. Weigh it down using something such as dried beans to keep it flat. Bake until golden (15 min.). Carefully remove the parchment and pie weights and bake ten

minutes more. Cool it while making the pie filling.
4. Adjust the oven temperature to 325° Fahrenheit.
5. Whisk the eggs and sugar in a large mixing container.
6. Melt and add the butter, milk, vinegar, and vanilla, whisking until incorporated. Mix in the cornmeal, flour, and salt until combined.
7. Dump the filling into the pie crust and bake until just set in the middle (50 min.). Cool the pie at room temperature for at least four hours. Then, pop it into the fridge until ready to serve.
8. Dust with powdered sugar before serving.

Coconut Cream Pie Bars

Servings Provided: 15 - varies
Time Required: 60 minutes + chill time

Ingredients Needed:

Crust Ingredients:
- Butter (1cup/2 sticks)
- A-P flour (2 cups)
- Powdered sugar (.5 cup)

Filling Ingredients:
- Half-and-Half (3 cups)
- Eggs (4)
- Coconut milk (3 cups)
- White sugar (1.5 cups)
- Salt (.5 tsp.)
- Cornstarch (.66 cup)
- Flaked coconut (1.5 cups)
- Coconut extract (.5 tsp.)
- Vanilla extract (.5 tsp.)

Topping Ingredients:
- Heavy whipping cream (2 cups)
- Water (1 tbsp. - cold)
- Gelatin (1 tsp.)
- Powdered sugar (3-4 tbsp.)
- Coconut - for toasting (1 cup)
- Also Needed: 9 x 13-inch baking dish

Preparation Technique:

1. Make the crust. Warm the oven at 350° Fahrenheit. Prepare the baking dish with a foil sling (if desired).
2. Combine the powdered sugar and flour. Dice and mix in the butter using a food processor (pulse it about 6-10 times) and press the mixture into the pan. Bake until light brown (18-20 min.) and cool it on a wire rack.
3. Toast the coconut. Spread one cup of the coconut flakes onto a baking tray and bake in the oven along with your shortbread crust for three to six minutes, stirring every minute or so until the coconut is golden brown. Spread it out on a plate to thoroughly cool.
4. Prepare the cream filling. Whisk the coconut milk, half-and-half, eggs, sugar, cornstarch, and salt in a large saucepan. Once boiling, adjust the temperature setting to med-low, whisking c until it's thick and bubbling (15-30 min.).
5. Add in the coconut and vanilla extracts and the 1.5 cups of untoasted coconut. Stir and dump the filling over the crust. Cool it on the countertop a short time and pop it into the refrigerator to chill about two to four hours until it's firm.
6. Prepare the topping. Measure and add one tablespoon cold water in a small bowl and sprinkle the gelatin evenly over the top. Let it soften for two minutes before microwaving it

for 30 seconds and whisking to dissolve the gelatin.
7. Use a chilled bowl and beater to whisk two cups of heavy cream and powdered sugar until the cream forms stiff peaks. Stop and add the gelatin mixture about halfway through.
8. Plop the cream over the bars and gently spread it around. Sprinkle on toasted coconut.
9. Pop it into the fridge to chill until serving time. Pull the bars out of the dish by slicing with a sharp knife to enjoy.

Creamy Hazelnut Pie

Servings Provided: 8
Time Required: 10 minutes + chill time

Ingredients Needed:

- Unchilled cream cheese (8 oz. pkg.)
- Confectioner's sugar (1 cup)
- Nutella - divided (1.25 cups)
- Thawed - frozen whipped topping (8 oz. carton)
- Chocolate crumb 9-inch crust

Preparation Technique:

1. Cream the sugar, cream cheese, one cup of Nutella, and the confectioner's sugar.
2. Fold in the topping and add the mixture to the crust.
3. Warm the rest of the Nutella in a microwave for 15-20 seconds and drizzle it over the pie.
4. Pop the pie into the fridge for at least four hours or overnight for the best results.

The Famous Woolworth Ice Box Cheesecake

Servings Provided: 6
Time Required: 10 minutes + chill time

Ingredients Needed:

- Lemon Jell-O (3 oz. pkg.)
- Boiling water (1 cup)
- Cream cheese (8 oz.)
- Granulated sugar (1 cup)
- Lemon juice (5 tbsp.)
- Evaporated milk - well chilled - ex. Carnation (12 oz. can)
- Graham crackers - crushed
- Also Needed: 9 by 13-inch baking pan

Preparation Technique:

1. Dissolve Jell-O in boiling water. Cool slightly until it's thickened.
2. Combine the cream cheese, sugar, and lemon juice with an electric mixer until smooth. Add in the thickened Jell-O and mix.
3. In another container, beat the milk until fluffy. Add the cream cheese mixture and blend well using the mixer.
4. Line the baking tray with crushed crackers.
5. Dump the filling into the pan and top with more crushed crackers and chill.

Frozen Banana Split Pie

Servings Provided: 8
Time Required: 25 minutes + chill time

Ingredients Needed:

- Hard-shell ice cream topping - chocolate (3 tbsp.)
- Graham cracker crust (1 - 9-inch)
- Bananas (2 medium)
- Lemon juice (.5 tsp.)
- Pineapple ice cream topping (.5 cup)
- Softened strawberry ice cream (1 quart)
- Whipped topping (2 cups)
- Toasted walnuts (.5 cup - chopped)
- Chocolate syrup
- Maraschino cherries with stems (8)

Preparation Technique:

1. Pour the chocolate topping into the crust and pop it into the freezer until chocolate is solid (5 min.).
2. Slice and arrange the bananas in a bowl to toss with the juice.
3. Place the bananas over the chocolate topping and layer using the pineapples, ice cream, whipped topping, and chopped nuts.
4. Use a layer of plastic to cover the pie and freeze it until firm. Transfer it to the countertop to thaw for about 15 minutes before slicing it to serve.

5. Top it off using the chocolate syrup and stemmed cherries.

Frozen Peach Pie

Servings Provided: 8/2 pies
Time Required: 30 minutes + freeze time

Ingredients Needed:

- Graham cracker crumbs (2.5 cups)
- Melted butter - divided (.5 cup + 2 tbsp.)
- Sugar (.25 cup)
- Sweetened condensed milk (14 oz. can)
- Orange juice (.25 cup)
- Lemon juice (.25 cup)
- Frozen unsweetened sliced peaches (16 oz. pkg.)
- Grated lemon zest (1 tbsp.)
- Heavy whipping cream (1.5 cups)
- Optional: Sweetened whipped cream (as desired)
- Also Needed: 2 greased 9-inch pie plates

Preparation Technique:

1. Warm the oven at 350° Fahrenheit.
2. Crumble and combine the cracker crumbs, sugar, and butter onto the bottom and up the sides of the two pie plates. Bake the pies until lightly browned (10-12 min.). Cool on wire racks.
3. Measure and add the milk, lemon juice, orange juice, peaches, and lemon zest into a blender and mix until smooth. Dump it into a mixing container.

4. In another container, beat the cream until stiff peaks form and fold it into the peach mixture.
5. Scoop the filling into the crusts. Cover and freeze for at least four hours or until firm.
6. Transfer the delicious pie to the table about 15 minutes before serving and top with whipped cream if desired.

Key Lime Pie

Servings Provided: 8
Time Required: 20 minutes + chill time

Ingredients Needed:

- Boiling water (.25 cup)
- Sugar-free lime gelatin (0.3 oz. pkg.)
- Key lime yogurt (2 - 6 oz. cartons)
- Reduced-fat graham cracker crust (6 oz.)
- Frozen fat-free whipped topping (8 oz. carton)

Preparation Technique:

1. Boil the water and add it to the gelatin. Stir for about two minutes until it's dissolved.
2. Whisk in the yogurt and topping.
3. Pour it into the crust and pop in the fridge.
4. Chill the pie for at least two hours and serve.

Strawberry Lemonade Freezer Pie

Servings Provided: 8
Time Required: 15 minutes + freeze time

Ingredients Needed:

- Frozen & thawed - sliced sweet strawberries (23.2 oz. container/2.5 cups)
- Instant lemon pudding mix (3.4 oz. pkg.)
- Frozen - thawed whipped topping (8 oz. cartons)
- Graham cracker crust (6 oz./9-inch)
- Optional: Additional fresh berries & whipped topping

Preparation Technique:

1. Combine the strawberries (with juices) and pudding mix in a large mixing container.
2. Wait for about five minutes and fold in the whipped topping.
3. Spread the filling into the crust.
4. Freeze the pie for at least eight hours to overnight. Let it stand for five to ten minutes before serving.

Sweet Potato Pie

Servings Provided: 8
Time Required: 2 hours – varies

Ingredients Needed:

- A-P flour (1.25 cups + more for dusting)
- Leaf lard (4 tbsp.)
- Good-quality butter (4 tbsp.)
- Kosher salt (.25 tsp.)
- Ice water (3-4 tbsp.)

  The Potato Filling:

- Orange-fleshed California sweet potatoes (2 large/about 1.75 lb.)
- White sugar (.5 cup)
- Large eggs (2 lightly whisked0
- Half & Half - heavy cream (.25 cup)
- Cinnamon (.75 tsp.)
- Nutmeg - freshly grated (.25 tsp.)
- Light brown sugar (.5 cup - packed)
- Unsalted butter (7 tbsp.)
- Kosher salt

Preparation Technique:

1. Cut the butter and lard into small pieces. Mix each of the dough components (omit the water) in a large mixing container. Knead the mixture until crumbly with a few lumps in it.
2. Drizzle the mixture using the ice water and work the dough.

3. Shape the dough and wrap it in plastic wrap to chill it for one hour. When cold, scoop the dough onto a well-floured surface. Dust flour over the top. Knead the dough, adding flour as needed.
4. Work the dough until it will extend over the edges of the pie pan.
5. Warm the oven at 400° Fahrenheit.
6. 'Blind-bake' the pie dough for 15 minutes. Thoroughly cool it in the pan on a rack for about half an hour. Lower the oven temperature to 350° Fahrenheit.
7. Make the filling. Warm a pot of water using the high-temperature setting. Peel and slice the potatoes into one-inch cubes. Lower the setting to medium and toss in the potatoes to cook until (20 to 25 min.). Drain and rinse using cold water.
8. Toss them into a food processor to create a creamy purée. Measure and return 2.5 cups into the food processor. Whisk and add the eggs, butter, granulated sugar, half-and-half, nutmeg, cinnamon, and brown sugar. Mix until smooth and dump into the pie shell, smoothing the top.
9. Place the pie pan on a baking sheet and set a timer to bake until the crust is lightly golden and filling is almost set with a slight jiggle in the center (1 hr.).
10. Cool thoroughly on a wire rack. Place a layer of foil over the pie and pop in the fridge until it's time to serve.

Chapter 13: Cake Favorites

Blueberry Sour Cream Pound Cake

Servings Provided: 12
Time Required: 1 hour 35 minutes

Ingredients Needed:

- A-P flour - divided (3 cups + 2 tbsp.)
- Baking soda (.5 tsp.)
- Sugar (3 cups)
- Salt (.5 tsp.)
- Unchilled - unsalted butter (1 cup or 2 sticks)
- Sour cream (1 cup)
- Eggs (6)
- Vanilla (1 tsp.)
- Blueberries (2 cups)
- To Dust: Powdered sugar

Preparation Technique:

1. Set the oven temperature setting at 325° Fahrenheit. Butter and flour a bundt pan.
2. Sift/whisk three cups of flour, salt, and baking soda to remove lumps. Set it to the side for now.
3. Mix the sugar and butter using an electric mixer until it is creamy. Add in sour cream and beat until it's combined.

4. Alternate adding flour mixture and eggs, beating until just combined. Quickly mix in the vanilla.
5. Gently toss the blueberries and two tablespoons flour. Fold the blueberries into the batter.
6. Dump the batter into the prepared pan and bake until golden and a toothpick inserted into the center comes out clean (1 ¼ hr.).
7. Cool it in the bundt pan for at least ten minutes before turning onto a wire rack to cool completely.
8. Once cool, dust it using a bit of powdered sugar.

Carrot Cake Delight

Servings Provided: 2 - 10-inch rounds
Time Required: 2 hours 25 minutes

Ingredients Needed:

- Grated carrots (6 cups)
- Raisins (1 cup)
- Brown sugar (1 cup)
- Eggs (4)
- White sugar (1.5 cups)
- Vegetable oil (1 cup)
- Vanilla extract (2 tsp.)
- Drained crushed pineapple (1 cup)
- Salt (1 tsp.)
- A-P flour (3 cups)
- Baking soda (1.5 tsp.)
- Ground cinnamon (4 tsp.)
- Chopped walnuts (1 cup)

Preparation Technique:

1. Grate the carrots and mix with the brown sugar. Set aside for about one hour and stir in the raisins.
2. Warm the oven at 350° Fahrenheit. Grease and flour the cake pans.
3. Whisk the eggs until light and mix in the white sugar, vanilla, and oil. Fold in the pineapple.
4. Sift or whisk the flour, cinnamon, baking soda, and salt, and fold into the wet mixture until

absorbed. Lastly, fold in the carrot mixture and nuts. Pour into the prepared pans.
5. Bake for 45 to 50 minutes until the cake tests are completed using a toothpick. (Stick the center of the cakes; when done, it's clean. Transfer the pans to the countertop to cool for ten minutes before removing from the pan.
6. Wait for them to cool to frost with frosting and serve.

Four Layer Pumpkin Cake With Frosting

Servings Provided: 16
Time Required: 1.5 hours

Ingredients Needed:

- Fine sea salt (.5 tsp.)
- A-P flour (3 cups)
- Baking powder (2 tsp.)
- Chinese five-spice powder (1 tsp.)
- Baking soda (1 tsp.)
- Unchilled - unsalted butter (2 sticks)
- Golden brown sugar - packed (2 cups)
- Unchilled eggs (3 large)
- Pure pumpkin (15-oz. can)
- Whole milk (.33 cup)

   The Icing:

- Unsalted - unchilled butter (1 cup)
- Unchilled cream cheese (2 ½ - 8-oz. pkg.)
- Orange peel - finely grated (1 tbsp.)
- Powdered sugar - sifted (3 cups)
- Orange juice (.25 cup)
- Walnut halves/chopped - toasted
- Also Needed: 2 cake pans - 9-inch with 1.5-inch sides
- Cooking oil spray (as needed)

Preparation Technique:

1. Position the rack in the bottom third of the oven, warming it to reach 350° Fahrenheit. Spray the pans using a spritz of baking oil spray. Line the bottoms using a layer of parchment baking paper (lightly greasing the paper too).
2. Whisk the baking powder and soda, flour, salt, and 5-spice powder.
   Use an electric mixer to combine the butter and brown sugar in another large bowl until creamy. Mix in the eggs one at a time.
   Fold in the pumpkin and dry fixings in three additions - alternately with milk in two additions. Dump the prepared batter into the baking trays.
3. Bake the cakes until the tester inserted into the center comes out clean (40 min.). Cool in pans on a rack for about 15 minutes. Loosen the edges with a small spatula and invert the cakes on cooling racks. Remove the parchment. Flip the cakes over onto racks and leave until thoroughly cooled.
4. Prepare the frosting using an electric mixer to mix the butter in a large mixing container until smooth. Mix in the cream cheese and orange peel, beating until creamy. Fold in and mix the powdered sugar (low speed).
5. Trim the rounded tops from cakes. Use a long serrated knife to cut each cake horizontally in half. Arrange one cake layer, cut side up, onto a large platter.

6. Spoon about 2/3 cup of frosting onto the cake - spreading to the edges.
7. Continue two more times with the cake and frosting. Top with the remaining cake layer with the cut side down. Decorate it using the rest of the frosting.
8. Top it off using walnuts before serving.

Georgia Peach Pound Cake

Servings Provided: 8
Time Required: 1 hour 20 minutes

Ingredients Needed:

- Eggs (4)
- Softened butter/margarine (1 cup)
- A-P flour (3 cups)
- White sugar (2 cups)
- Salt (.5 tsp.)
- Baking powder (1 tsp.)
- Vanilla extract (1 tsp.)
- Fresh peaches (2 cups - pitted & chopped)

Preparation Technique:

1. Set the oven at 325°Fahrenheit. Butter a ten-inch tube pan and sprinkle with white sugar.
2. Cream the sugar with the butter until it's fluffy. Whisk and fold in the eggs - one at a time - whisking after each addition. Mix in the vanilla.
3. Set aside ¼ of a cup of flour for later, and sift the rest of the flour with the baking powder and salt. Slowly mix it into the creamed mixture.
4. Toss the reserved flour over the chopped peaches, and mix thoroughly into the batter. Dump the batter into the prepared pan.
5. Bake the cake for one hour and about 15 minutes.

6. Leave the cake in the pan for about ten minutes, before placing it onto a wire rack to cool completely.
7. For the sauce, puree a portion of the peaches, add two tablespoon cornstarch, and cook using the low-temperature setting until thickened. Serve the mixture as a sauce over the cake.

Pineapple Pecan Cake With Frosting

Servings Provided: 8
Time Required: 40-45 minutes

Ingredients Needed:

The Cake:
- Sugar (2 cups)
- Baking soda (2 tsp.)
- Flour (2 cups)
- Eggs (2)
- Crushed pineapple with juice (20-oz. can)
- Optional: Chopped pecans (1 cup) *The Icing*:

- Unchilled - softened butter (1 stick)
- Cream cheese - softened (8-oz. pkg.)
- Confectioners sugar (2 cups)
- Vanilla (1 tbsp.)
- Also Needed: 9x13-inch baking pan

Preparation Technique:

1. Whisk the sugar, flour, and baking soda in a large mixing container. Butter the baking pan and set the oven temperature setting at 350°Fahrenheit.
2. Whisk and mix in the eggs, pineapple, and juice with the pecans. Mix just until moistened.
3. Dump the batter into the buttered pan. Set the timer to bake until done (30-35 min.). Transfer

it to the countertop and wait for it to cool thoroughly.
4. Prepare the icing by combining the butter, cream cheese, vanilla, and confectioners sugar. Beat until smooth.
5. Decorate the cake and serve.

Red Velvet Cake

Servings Provided: 6-inch cake
Time Required: 50 minutes

Ingredients Needed:

The Cake:
- A-P flour (1.25 cups)
- Baking soda (.75 tsp.)
- Unsweetened cocoa powder (1 tbsp.)
- Kosher salt (.5 tsp.)
- Coconut oil (.5 cup)
- Sugar (1 cup)
- Egg (1 large)
- Red food coloring (1 tbsp.)
- Vinegar (.5 tsp.)
- Vanilla bean paste/extract (1.5 tsp.)
- Buttermilk (.5 cup) *The Frosting:*

- Unchilled - unsalted butter (.5 cup)
- Unchilled - cream cheese (4 oz.)
- Powdered sugar (2 cups)
- Vanilla bean paste or extract (1 tsp.)
- Kosher salt (1/8 tsp.) *Also Needed*:
- Two 6-inch round cake pans
- Stand mixer fitted with a paddle attachment

Preparation Technique:

1. Warm the oven to 350° Fahrenheit. Lightly grease the pans and set them aside for now.

2. Whisk the salt, flour, baking soda, and cocoa powder.
3. Prepare the mixer. Cream the coconut oil and sugar until fluffy (3-4 min.). Whisk and add the egg, food coloring, vanilla, and vinegar.
4. Mix in the dry components and buttermilk in two to three alternating additions and beat until just combined.
5. Portion the batter between the cake pans and bake until a toothpick inserted into the center comes out clean (25 minutes).
6. Gently press down the top of the cakes to even them out while they're still hot. Cool them for ten minutes in their pans and turn them onto a wire rack to cool completely.
7. *Prepare the Frosting:* Cream the butter and cream cheese in the stand mixer until combined. Add in the salt, powdered sugar, and vanilla.
8. *To Assemble:* Stack up the cooled cake layers with a thick layer of frosting in between. Frost and serve.
9. *Note*: For the oil, unrefined provides a hint of coconut flavor or use refined for no coconut flavor.

Chapter 14: Other Sweet Goodies

American Patriotic Dessert Dish

Servings Provided: 20
Time Required: 4 hours 20 minutes

Ingredients Needed:

- Boiling water - divided (4 cups)
- Jell-O Gelatin - red & blue (8-serving package - 1 of each)
- Water (2 cups - cold)
- Prepared pound cake cubes (4 cups)
- Cool Whip Topping - thawed (8 oz. tub.)
- Sliced strawberries (2 cups)

   Also Needed:

- Baking pans: 13x9-inch
- 3.5-quart serving dish

Preparation Technique:

1. Prepare two bowls. Stir two cups of boiling water into each flavor of dry gelatin using individual containers. It should take about two minutes for it to fully dissolve.
2. Stir one cup of cold water into each bowl. Pour each of the gelatins into separate pans. Pop them in the fridge for four (4) hours until firm. Slice the gelatin into half-inch cubes.

3. Prepare the layers in the serving bowl, starting with the red cubes, a layer of cake cubes, half of the topping, and the berries. Lastly, add the blue cubes and the rest of the whipped topping.
4. Place the delicious treat in the fridge to chill for a minimum of one hour or until ready to serve.

Banana Pudding

Servings Provided: 8
Time Required: 45 minutes

Ingredients Needed:

- Sugar (.5 cup + 2 tbsp.)
- A-P flour (.33 cup)
- 2% milk (2 cups)
- Eggs (3 separated)
- Vanilla extract (1 tsp.)
- Pinch of salt
- Large ripe bananas (4 sliced)
- Vanilla wafers (half of 12 oz. box/about 35 wafers)
- Also Needed: 8 by 8-inch baking dish

Preparation Technique:

1. Set the oven temperature at 375° Fahrenheit.
2. Combine the flour, 1/2 cup of sugar, milk, egg yolks, salt, and vanilla in a medium saucepan.
3. Simmer the mixture using the low-temperature setting, whisking occasionally until the mixture thickens into a pudding (12 min.).
4. Place the **egg whites** in a mixing bowl and beat with an electric mixer until thick and stiff peaks have formed.
5. Fold in two tablespoons of sugar and mix for another few seconds to incorporate.
6. Layer the bottom of the baking dish with half of the bananas, and top with half the cookies.

Repeat to form two layers of wafers and bananas. Lastly, pour the pudding over the top.
7. Spread the meringue over the pudding. Bake until the meringue is golden brown (10-12 min.).
8. Note: You can also whip the meringue by hand using a whisk in a cold aluminum mixing bowl; it's a workout!

Blackberry Cobbler

Servings Provided: 10-12
Time Required: 35 minutes

Ingredients Needed:

TheCobbler:
- Blackberries - fresh or frozen (6 to 8 cups)
- Granulated sugar (1.5 cups)
- A-P flour (.5 cup)
- Fresh lemon juice (2 tbsp.)
- Optional: Blackberry liqueur (1-2 tbsp.)

Biscuit Topping:

- A-P flour (2 cups)
- Baking powder (4 tsp.)
- Granulated sugar (3 tbsp.)
- Salt (1 tsp.)
- Lemon peel (zest of 1 lemon)
- Butter (.5 cup - chilled & cut into ¼-inch chunks
- Milk (2/3 cup)
- Egg (1 slightly beaten)

Preparation Technique:

1. Warm the oven to reach 400° Fahrenheit. If you want to make cleaning up easier, cover a baking tray using a layer of foil to catch the drippings and juice that usually boils over from the container as it cooks.

2. Wash, remove the stems and drain fresh berries.
3. Toss the flour, sugar, blackberries, blackberry liqueur, and lemon juice. Pour into the prepared baking dish or skillet.
4. Prepare the biscuit topping and set it aside until ready to use.
5. Bake the blackberry cobbler (without the topping), uncovered, approximately 15 to 20 minutes or until hot and bubbly.
6. When the blackberry mixture is hot, remove from the oven and spoon the prepared topping mixture onto the top in 10-12 large spoonfuls, which is a marker for each serving.
7. Transfer the pan to the oven and bake the cobbler until biscuits are lightly browned (20-25 min.).
8. Transfer the pan to a wire rack to chill for at least ten minutes before it's time to serve with a portion of vanilla ice cream if desired.

Blueberry-Peach Cobbler

Servings Provided: 6
Time Required: 35 minutes

Ingredients Needed:

- Peaches (2 lb.)
- Blueberries (1 cup)
- Sugar (.25 cup + 2 tbsp.)
- Cornstarch (2 tsp.)
- Juice (half of 1 lemon)
- All-purpose flour (1 cup)
- Cold butter (4 tbsp.)
- Baking powder (.75 tsp.)
- Salt (.25 tsp.)
- Baking soda (.25 tsp.)
- Plain 2% Greek yogurt (.33 cup)
- Brown sugar (1 tbsp.)
- Also Needed 8 by 8-inch baking dish

Preparation Technique:

1. Warm the oven at 350° Fahrenheit.
2. Peel and slice each peach into six wedges. Gently combine the blueberries, peaches, ¼ cup of sugar, cornstarch, a dash of salt, and lemon juice into the baking dish.
3. Mix thoroughly with a large spoon.
4. Dice the butter into cubes. Combine two tablespoons of sugar with the salt, flour, baking powder, and baking soda in a mixing container.

5. Break the butter in with the flour until it's a coarse meal.
6. Fold in the yogurt to create a shaggy dough, don't overmix. Portion the dough into six equal mounds.
7. Arrange the mounds over the peaches and sprinkle them using the brown sugar.
8. Set a timer to bake until the peaches are bubbling and the biscuits are golden brown (20 min.).

Grandma's Divinity

Servings Provided: 1.5 lb./60 pieces
Time Required: 45 minutes + wait time

Ingredients Needed:

- Egg whites (2 large)
- Water (.66 cup)
- Sugar (3 cups)
- Vanilla extract (1 tsp.)
- Light corn syrup (.5 cup)
- Pecans (1 cup - chopped)
- Also Needed: Three 15 by 10 by 1-inch pans

Preparation Technique:

1. Separate the eggs and toss the whites in the bowl of a stand mixer. Wait about half an hour - undisturbed - until they are room temperature.
2. Cover the pans with waxed paper.
3. Prepare a large, heavy saucepan to combine the corn syrup, water, and sugar, stirring until the sugar is dissolved.
4. Continue to cook - *not stirring* - using the medium temperature setting to reach a hard-ball stage (a candy thermometer reads 252° Fahrenheit). Right before the temperature is reached, whisk the egg whites using the medium speed to shape stiff peaks.
5. Slowly dump the hot sugar mixture over the egg whites, beating constantly. Stir in the vanilla and beat until candy holds its shape or

about five to six minutes. Promptly, mix in the pecans.
6. Drop by heaping teaspoonfuls onto the pans to rest until they are dry to touch.
7. Place into containers using waxed paper in between the layers. Store them in the pantry in a closed container and enjoy the treats as desired.

Honey-Baked Apples

Servings Provided: 2
Time Required: 45 minutes

Ingredients Needed:

- Tart apples (2 medium)
- Dried cranberries (.25 cup)
- Water (2/3 cup)
- Also Needed: 8x4-inch glass loaf pan

Preparation Technique:

1. Set the oven temperature at 350° Fahrenheit.
2. Core the apples, leaving the bottoms intact; peel the top third of each. Arrange them in the greased pan and fill it with cranberries.
3. Prepare a saucepan and add the water, brown sugar, and honey. Simmer the mixture using the medium temperature setting to dissolve the sugar and dump it over the apples.
4. Bake until the apples are tender while basting with their natural juices (35 min.).
5. Place the apples in serving dishes with a scoop of ice cream if desired.

Pumpkin Butterscotch Pudding

Servings Provided: 6
Time Required: 20 minutes + chill time

Ingredients Needed:

- Sugar (1 cup)
- Dark brown sugar - packed (.5 cup)
- Cornstarch (3 tbsp.)
- Salt (.25 tsp.)
- Ground nutmeg (.125 tsp.)
- 2% milk (3 cups)
- Cubed butter (2 tbsp.)
- Egg yolks (3)
- Vanilla extract (2 tsp.)
- Optional: Whipped cream

Preparation Technique:

1. Combine both sugars, cornstarch, nutmeg, and salt. Add them to a saucepan and stir in the milk. Simmer the mixture using the med-high temperature setting until thickened and bubbly.
2. Adjust the setting to low, and cook while stirring for two more minutes. Transfer the pan to a cool burner.
3. Stir a bit of hot mixture into the egg yolks and return all of the mixture back into the pan. Simmer at a gentle boil for about two minutes or until the mixture is thickened and coats the back of a spoon. Place the pan on the countertop and mix in the butter and vanilla.

Cool the pudding for 15 minutes, stirring occasionally.
4. Pour it into six dessert dishes. Pop them in the fridge until chilled.
5. Serve with a garnish of whipped cream if desired.

Tennessee Peach Pudding

Servings Provided: 8
Time Required: 1 hour

Ingredients Needed:

- A-P flour (1 cup)
- Sugar (.5 cup)
- Salt (.5 tsp.)
- Baking powder (2 tsp.)
- Optional: Cinnamon (.5 tsp.)
- 2% milk (.5 cup)
- Fresh/frozen peaches (3 cups) *The Topping*:
- Brown sugar (.5 cup - packed)
- Water (1.5 cups)
- Sugar (.5 cup)
- Butter (1 tbsp.)
- Ground nutmeg (.25 tsp.)
- Optional: Vanilla ice cream
- Also Needed: 8-inch square baking dish

Preparation Technique:

1. Set the oven temperature at 400° Fahrenheit. Whisk or sift the flour, salt, sugar, cinnamon, and baking powder.
2. Stir in the milk - just until combined. Peel and slice the peaches and fold them into the mixture. Dump them into the greased baking dish.

3. Prepare the topping by mixing the water, butter, sugars, and nutmeg in a large saucepan. Boil and stir until the sugars are dissolved, and dump the mixture over the peaches.
4. Bake until filling is bubbly (40-50 min.). Serve warm or chilled with ice cream - as desired.

Conclusion

I hope you have enjoyed each delicious recipe in *American Cuisine*. All you need to do is follow the guidelines, and you will enjoy all the country's cuisine has to offer. The next step is to decide which meal or sweet treat you will prepare first; there are so many!

I believe we have you ready to start creating your new American masterpiece meal, so here are the additional tips offered to keep you on target and provide you with tons of suggestions to help you become a top baker or chef!

1. Have fun while you enjoy your new recipes, remembering they are merely suggestions that have worked for other chefs or bakers. You can always use substitutions to indulge a unique diet or your personal choices.

2. Consider meal prep to keep your deliciously prepared meals fresh and provide a huge variety using the new array of recipes.

3. Prepare the area where you will be working. Gather all of the tools needed, including bowls, spoons, measuring cups, etc. Have a trashcan handy and keep the area clear of 'trash.'

4. Always thoroughly read and reread your recipes before you start cooking.

5. Always carefully measure when baking bread or other similar delicate recipes. It is a science to make the bread rise correctly, and any wrong measurements can be disastrous.

6. You may have the need to use an egg wash. It is a simple process created by whisking one tablespoon of water with a large egg until it's smooth. When used over pastries for sealing, it will also provide a glossy appearance.

7. Easily prepare tomatoes by making an 'x' in its top. Place it in a saucepan of boiling water for about half of a minute. Let it cool, and you can easily remove the skin.

8. Use salt to perk up a 'dull' recipe. It will enhance the flavor out of your dishes. Most of the recipes you prepare are using kosher salt and sea salt (a bit pricier) for an additional kick.

9. If you love boiled eggs but hate the messy shells, simply place a layer of paper towels on the countertop and break them apart over it. Toss the mess!

10. Make a standard rule after preparing a tasty dish; perform a taste test of the prepared item, such as fried chicken, so you don't ruin its intended flavor potential.

11. If you have trouble keeping your cutting board steady, dampen a paper towel and place it underneath it. (Problem solved!)

12. One of the most functional tools for meal preparation is a sharp chef's knife. Invest in a good-quality one that will last for years. Have you ever tried to filet a fish using a dull knife?

13. Owning a super-sharp knife is wonderful, but you must know how to properly handle it while you are slicing your favorite steak. The professionals indicate it is much safer to 'pinch the blade' instead of gripping the handle. It is proclaimed to be a safer practice. (Maybe it is worth a try; it makes sense!)

14. Many of the recipes will require or suggest using a cast-iron skillet. It helps to evenly cook your meals and easily cleaned.

15. If you enjoy preparing a fresh salad, grasp the stem with one hand, and gently pull the leaf with the other, so you do not bruise the leaves.

16. Keep your spices away from heat sources, such as the stovetop or on shelves near light sources. The quality of spices and herbs diminishes and can lose their flavor when exposed to heat and humidity.

17. Kitchen Essentials: If this is your first experience preparing specialty foods in your kitchen, you will want to purchase eggs, milk, all-purpose (A-P) flour, extra-virgin olive oil, soy sauce, sugar, salt, black pepper, broth (chicken & beef if desired), pasta, brown rice, and a variety of beans. These are good starters,

but each recipe will provide you with essential items needed.

18. If you love freshly peeled apples but hate how they quickly turn brown; lightly spritz them using a portion of fresh lime or lemon juice after they are prepared as desired.

19. Honey is a favorite American complement to dishes in place of sugar or other sweeteners. It also never spoils and is a natural preservative.

20. Consider making your own breadcrumbs using a food processor. Reserve your stale bread to prepare a stash using your favorite recipe. Pop them into the freezer and enjoy them for up to six months.

21. Wait for your steaks to reach room temperature before seasoning and grilling. In theory, you want the meat to cook evenly from edge to center. Therefore, the closer it is to its final eating temperature, the more evenly it will cook. Letting it sit on the counter for 20 to 30 minutes will bring the steak up to room temperature—a good 20 to 25° Fahrenheit closer to your final serving temperature.

22. If you have opened bags of flour and cornmeal, store them in the freezer compartment to extend the life of each product.

23. Purchase butter when it's on sale and pop it into the freezer for longer shelf life (up to six months).

24. Save the box of brown sugar that has hardened in the cabinet. Pop it into a zipper-type baggie and add a slice of bread. Let it rest overnight, and you will be surprised at the results in the morning!

25. If you are an avocado lover and don't use the entire one, just leave the pit in the saved half and pop it in the fridge to use another day. It will help it remain fresh.

26. If you want to place your veggies in a pan upright, such as an onion, just chop off one end and place it into the pan.

27. You can rehydrate sun-dried tomatoes by soaking them in hot water or stock for (20-25 min.).

28. Always store your garlic on the countertop or unchilled to prevent it from becoming rancid.

29. You have prepared a batch of tomato paste and have leftovers. Just scoop it into ice cube trays and pop them in the freezer for your next recipe.

30. Some of the bread recipes (in particular) require you to soften butter. This is easily accomplished by placing the dish of butter on the countertop and chopping it into small slices for about 10 to 15 minutes.

I hope these tips will help you enjoy all of your new 'favorite' dishes. Finally, if you found this book useful in any way, a review is always appreciated!

"Other books by Arsenio Islas"

Copycat Cookbook: *Japanese Cuisine: 100+ Delicious, Quick and Easy Recipes to Follow to Prepare your Favorite Dishes at the Home Restaurant. Including Cooking Techniques for Beginners*

Copycat Recipes Cookbook: *Thai Cuisine 100+ Tasty Recipes. The Complete Step-By-Step Guide to Cooking Delicious Dishes, from Appetizers to Desserts*

Copycat Recipes: *Mexican Cuisine 100+ Delicious, Quick and Easy Recipes, Including Cooking Techniques for Beginners, From Appetizers to Desserts*

Copycat: 4 Manuscripts: American Cuisine Japanese Cuisine Thai Cuisine Mexican Cuisine

CPSIA information can be obtained
at www.ICGtesting.com
Printed in the USA
BVHW081542181120
593626BV00007B/468